READING

English Reading Programme

3rd Class

The Talking Horse

STORIES • NON-FICTION • ACTIVITIES

FOLENS

Author: Trina Cooney
Editor: Sarah Deegan
Design: Liz White Designs
Layout: Niamh Carey
Illustrators: Eoin Cooney, Diarmuid Cooney, Martin Pierce, Kim Shaw, Dave Peet, Peter Wilks (SGA) and Steph Dix, Bridget Dowty, Leighton Noyes, Emily Skinner, James Walmesley and Sue Woollatt (GCI)
Cover Illustration: Kim Shaw
Cover Design: Liz White Designs
ISBN: 978-1-84741-216-4

Introduction to Teachers and Parents

Reading Zone is an innovative and contemporary Reading series that was written by Irish primary teachers.

The Senior Level of *Reading Zone* has four books for third to sixth class. There are thirty units in each book; twenty-two story units and eight non-fiction units. Each unit also has activities based on the text.

The story units have very engaging short stories whose length has been kept to a minimum. The stories are interspersed with a few 'stand alone' extracts from the novels of popular writers as well as much-loved classics. Also featured are tales by Hans Christian Anderson and Aesop's fables.

The eight non-fiction units are interesting and relevant, covering themes such as adventure sports, web sites, catalogues, recipes, newspaper articles and nature.

Each unit is designed to last for approximately one week. The text of the stories is divided into small sections to facilitate the assignment of homework or other activities. Pre-reading vocabulary work can be carried out on the highlighted words in the text. Familiarity with these words prior to reading the text will assist the flow of reading and increase the pupil's confidence.

Each unit has an activity section with different types of activities. The activities cover literal comprehension, multiple choice questions, cloze procedure, interpretive comprehension, grammar, character description, exploring the text, creative thinking and summarising.

A boxed set of **30 parallel reading books** (fiction and non-fiction) is available for each class level. The books can be used independently of the Reading Zone series but extracts from the books are included in the readers. Each parallel book is accompanied by an activity card with factual multiple choice questions and activities based on the book. An answer card is also provided.

There is also an **oral and aural language programme** available for each class level. Each level contains CDs and a teacher's manual with forty lesson plans and accompanying photocopiables.

Acknowledgements

The publishers wish to thank Dublin Zoo for permission to reproduce material from their website.

Photographs: Dolphin © ImageState/Alamy. Whales © imagebroker/Alamy. Arctic hare © Visual&Written SL/Alamy. Chinese calendar © Helene Rogers/Alamy. Caterpillar © Carrie Garcia/Alamy. Frog © Redmond Durrell/Alamy. Nymph and Locust © Nigel Cattlin/Alamy. In-line Skaters © Stock Connection Distribution/Alamy. Girl jumping © Life File Photo Library Ltd/Alamy. Trampoline © Nicholas Eveleigh/Alamy.

Thanks to Karen Andrews, Rodolfo Belloli, Stacy Braswell, Chris Chidsey, Leo Cummings, Tibor Fazakas, John Foliot, Joe Glasgow, hortongrou, ijsendoorn, Vjeran Lisjak, Svetlana Maksimovic, netsemblance, Thomas Picard, Richard Redmerski, Miguel Saavedra, Mike Scott, Andrew Smith, Eric Stapleton, Ove Tøpfer, Mario Alberto Magallanes Trejo, Brith-Marie Warn, Ginny Warner, yenhoon and Musyahidah Zawawi (Stock.xchng) and Curt Pickens, farotechM, oneclearvision and Gary Sludden (iStockphoto)

Stories by Trina Cooney: 'Bear and Turtle Have a Race', 'The Talking Horse' (adapted from American folklore), 'The Wizard's Contest', 'Brave Hans', 'Jakub and the Kaha Bird' (adapted from European folklore), 'The Little Fir Tree' (adapted from Hans Christian Andersen), 'How Fionn Became Leader of the Fianna', 'Tamlin's Rescue' (adapted from Scottish folklore), 'The Dreamer', 'The Scarlet Rose' (adapted from Russian folklore), 'The Frog Prince', 'Clever Rosa' and 'A Lesson in Sharing'. Stories by Sarah Deegan: 'The Lion and the Rabbit' (adapted from an Indian folk tale) Stories by Donna Garvin: 'Dad, Sam and Blacky' (adapted from Aesop's Fable 'The Miller and the Donkey')

Hibernian Industrial Estate, Greenhills Road, Tallaght, Dublin 24
Produced by Folens Publishers

Contents

UNIT 1 The Lion and the Rabbit

Once upon a time there was a lion who liked to hunt. Every day he ran through the jungle hunting lots of different animals. The animals were not happy with this at all. They decided to call a meeting to see what they could do.

At noon, the animals all gathered where the banana trees grew. They arrived very quietly. They did not want to disturb the lion, who was sleeping under a tree. After much talking they thought of a plan. They decided that one animal would be sent to the lion every day for his dinner. In return, the lion would not hunt them ever again. They chose a group of animals to decide which animal would be the lion's dinner each day.

The gorilla was asked to tell the lion about the plan. That evening the gorilla met with the lion to tell him about their idea. The lion thought it over and because he was a lazy animal he decided that it was an excellent plan.

On the first day, a rabbit was chosen to be dinner for the lion. The rabbit was not at all pleased about this. She did not want to be eaten by the lion! She sat down and thought for a while. She made up a wonderful plan of her own!

When the time came for the rabbit to go to the lion, she hopped very slowly to the cave where he lived. When she got there the lion was angry.

"Why are you so late?" he roared, "I am very hungry!"

"Oh please don't be cross," said the rabbit.

"I didn't mean to be late. I was coming here to be your dinner when I was attacked by the other lion. I was lucky to escape!"

"Other lion?" asked the lion. He did not like the sound of this. "What other lion?"

"The one who lives quite near here," the rabbit said. "He is a very rude lion. He even said that you were not the king of the jungle!" The lion could not believe his ears. "How dare he?" roared the lion. "Bring me to him and I will show him that I am indeed the king of the jungle."

The rabbit bounded out of the cave followed closely by the proud lion. The little rabbit's plan was working. She led the lion to a deep well nearby.

"Is this where he lives?" asked the lion.

"Yes," replied the rabbit. "Look down into the well and you will see him."

"If he is hiding in this well," thought the lion, "maybe he is afraid of me!"

The lion moved towards the well. He looked down into the water and saw his own face. He thought it was another lion looking up at him. He roared at the lion. The lion roared back at him. He roared louder. The other lion roared louder too. The lion became furious. He jumped into the well to attack the other lion.

SPLASH!

The lion disappeared into the water and was never heard of again.

The rabbit went home feeling very pleased with herself.

UNIT 1 Activities

A Fact Finding

1. Where did the animals gather?
2. Who was asked to tell the lion about the plan?
3. Which animal was first to be chosen for the lion's dinner?
4. Where did the rabbit lead the lion?
5. What did the lion see in the water?

B Choose the word closest in meaning to the underlined word.

1. They **arrived** very quietly.
   (a) spoke (b) tiptoed
   (c) came (d) moved
2. They did not want to **disturb** the lion, who was sleeping under a tree.
   (a) help (b) amuse
   (c) annoy (d) comfort
3. It was an **excellent** plan.
   (a) brilliant (b) funny (c) ok (d) bad
4. The rabbit **bounded** out of the cave.
   (a) walked (b) hopped
   (c) skated (d) crawled
5. The lion became **furious**.
   (a) happy (b) lonely
   (c) sad (d) angry
6. He **disappeared** into the water.
   (a) melted (b) vanished
   (c) floated (d) bobbed

C Choose the most suitable word to complete each sentence.

1. They ________ that one animal would be sent to the lion each day. **(agreed, wrote, said, thought)**
2. That ________ the gorilla met with the lion. **(morning, afternoon, evening, night)**
3. The rabbit was not at all ________ about this. **(upset, happy, worried, annoyed)**
4. She led the lion to a deep well ________. **(far away, in the distance, close by, next door)**
5. The lion ________ to the well. **(walked, hopped, skated, danced)**
6. He jumped into the well to ________ the other lion. **(speak to, shout at, kill, fight with)**

D Choose the correct answer.

1. **Why did the animals decide to send the lion one animal every day?**
   (a) They thought he was lonely.
   (b) They were tired of being hunted.
   (c) He had asked them nicely.
   (d) He was king of the jungle.
2. **The rabbit hopped slowly to the lion's cave because**
   (a) she had a sore paw.
   (b) she was afraid.
   (c) it was part of her plan.
   (d) she did not know the way.
3. **Why did the lion follow the rabbit out of the cave?**
   (a) To see where she lived.
   (b) To have a walk before dinner.
   (c) To give out to the other lion.
   (d) To have a drink at the well.
4. **The lion saw his own face in the water and thought,**
   (a) "How handsome I am!"
   (b) "My nose is too big!"
   (c) "I must cut my hair!"
   (d) "That's another lion!"
5. **The rabbit went home very pleased with herself because**
   (a) she was still alive.
   (b) she had walked with the lion to the well.
   (c) she had escaped from the lion who had attacked her.
   (d) the sun was shining.

E Grammar

All sentences begin with a capital letter. People's names, place names, days of the week and months of the year also start with capital letters.

Rewrite these sentences using capital letters.

1. once upon a time there was a lion who liked to hunt.
2. the lion's name was sasha.
3. the animals met at noon on sunday.
4. "why are you so late?" sasha roared.
5. "yes," replied the rabbit. "look down the well and you will see him."
6. the lion was never heard of again and beauty the rabbit went home happily.

F Summarise

The rabbit made up a wonderful plan of her own. Read the rabbit's plan and rewrite it in your own words.

G Character Description

In this story we learn that the lion liked to hunt. We also learn that he was a lazy animal. Read the story again. Write a short paragraph describing the lion in your own words.

UNIT 2

Eat Your Veggies

From *Eat Your Vegies* by Jane C. Scott (Folens Reading Pack Level 3)

I don't like being small and I don't like vegetables. Every time we sit at the table for dinner, Mum says, "Eat your veggies, Jennifer."

And I say to Mum, "But I don't like veggies."

And she says, "They'll make you grow big and strong."

But I never seem to grow any bigger, so most of the time I try not to eat my veggies. But sometimes Mum gets really angry. Then I try to eat them, but the vegetables make me feel sick. So the best thing to do is to think up ways to hide them.

One night, I fed my broccoli to our dog, who was under the table. I dropped five big, green pieces of broccoli down there for her. But the dog didn't like broccoli either, so she just left them on the floor. I had to sneak them into the rubbish when Mum wasn't looking.

Another time, I tried putting five big chunks of pumpkin in my jeans pockets. I was going to empty them out after dinner when Mum wasn't looking. But

the pumpkin went all mushy and sticky and made a big orange mess in my pockets. Mum was mad!

I even tried to bribe my little sister to eat my veggies for me. She likes all kinds of vegetables. So I said I'd give her a euro if she ate mine too. She did it for two nights, but then Mum found out.

"Eat your own veggies, Jennifer!" she said sternly. "They'll make you grow big and strong."

But I wasn't going to eat the veggies, so I had to think up another wonderful idea. It was then that I noticed the plant. It's big and green with bright, bushy leaves that dangle down over the pot. And it sits next to our table right by where I sit! So, each night when Mum wasn't looking, I put my veggies in the plant's pot. Not even my sister or the dog saw me do it.

I put my veggies in there for five whole weeks and then the plant began to grow and grow. It got bigger and stronger and grew faster and faster. The more vegetables I gave it, the bigger and healthier it got. But the best thing of all was that I didn't have to eat broccoli, pumpkin, cabbage and all the rest of those vegetables any more. The plant ate them for me!

After a while I began to wonder. The plant was growing so big from eating vegetables. What if I ate them too? Maybe I would get big and strong!

UNIT 2

Activities

A Fact Finding

1. What two things did Jennifer not like?
2. What vegetable did Jennifer try to feed her dog?
3. Where did Jennifer hide the pumpkin?
4. How much money did Jennifer give her sister?
5. What happened to the plant?

B Choose the word closest in meaning to the underlined word.

1. I never **seem** to grow any bigger.
   (a) begin (b) appear
   (c) start (d) want
2. I had to **sneak** them into the rubbish.
   (a) slip (b) put (c) drop (d) place
3. I even tried to **bribe** my little sister to eat my veggies for me.
   (a) ask (b) beg (c) help (d) pay
4. So I had to think up another **wonderful** idea.
   (a) strange (b) great
   (c) awful (d) funny
5. Its bushy leaves **dangle** down over the pot.
   (a) drop (b) hang (c) flow (d) curl
6. After a while I began to **wonder**.
   (a) see (b) dream (c) think (d) ask

C Choose the most suitable word to complete each sentence.

1. But sometimes Mum gets really ________ . **(funny, happy, scary, cross)**
2. I tried putting five big ________ of pumpkin in my pockets. **(balls, seeds, flowers, pieces)**
3. "Eat your veggies," Mum says ________ . **(strictly, loudly, quietly, happily)**
4. Then I ________ the plant. **(found, heard, saw, dropped)**
5. The plant became bigger and ________ . **(thinner, stronger, weaker, brighter)**
6. "Maybe I could get big and strong if I ate my vegetables ________ ." **(now, as well, soon, later)**

D

Choose the correct answer.

1. **How does trying to eat veggies make Jennifer feel?**
   (a) Happy. (b) Unwell.
   (c) Sad. (d) Good.
2. **What did Jennifer do when the dog would not eat the broccoli?**
   (a) She hid it in the rubbish.
   (b) She hid it in her pocket.
   (c) She hid it in the sink.
   (d) She hid it in the pot.
3. **Jennifer's sister ate her veggies for two nights because**
   (a) she was asked to.
   (b) she liked them.
   (c) she had no choice.
   (d) she was paid.
4. **Why was the plant perfect for hiding the veggies?**
   (a) It was green.
   (b) It was big.
   (c) Its leaves dangled over the pot.
   (d) It was beside the table.
5. **After a while Jennifer began to wonder**
   (a) if the plant was too big.
   (b) where else to hide the veggies.
   (c) if she could grow big from eating veggies.
   (d) if the plant might explode.

E

Grammar

Capital letters are also used for the word I, days of the week and special days.

Rewrite these sentences using capital letters.

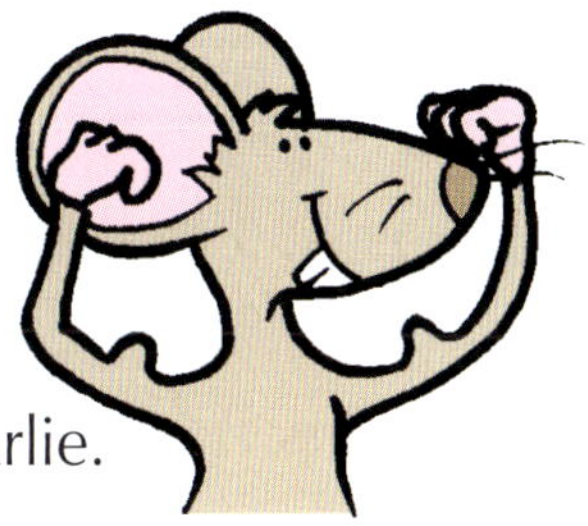

1. i don't like being small and i don't like vegetables.
2. jennifer's mother told her to eat her veggies.
3. "by hallowe'en, you will be big and strong," she said.
4. "on valentine's day i fed broccoli to our dog," said charlie.
5. my sister orla likes veggies so i said i would give her one euro if she ate mine too.
6. after a while I began to wonder if I might grow big and strong too!

F

Summarise

Jennifer did four different things with her veggies rather than eat them. Describe what she did in your own words.

G

Use Your Imagination

Mum was sorting the laundry. When she checked Jennifer's jeans she discovered a big orange mess in her pockets. Write the conversation between Mum and Jennifer.

UNIT 3

Queen Aleste Saves Prince Ikore

This story was written by Eoin Cooney when he was in Third Class in Primary School. He hopes you enjoy reading it. It was illustrated by Eoin and Diarmuid Cooney.

One fine morning, Queen Aleste of Mexico was out walking with her husband, King Jared. Suddenly a pineapple fell from one of the beautiful, tall trees in their huge garden.

The queen turned to her husband.

"Now, isn't that interesting?" she said. "That pineapple fell the second I stamped my foot on the ground."

Aleste was small and thin, quite the opposite of her husband. She had dark hair and blue eyes. She wasn't a very nice person and had many enemies.

Every time the queen stamped her foot a pineapple fell. She glanced up into the tree and saw her old enemy, El Diablo, hanging from one of the branches.

"I have captured Prince Ikore, your only son and heir to the throne, and I slipped some poison in your husband's drink. Oh and don't worry, I have a little surprise for you too," he snarled.

One week later King Jared was dead and Prince Ikore was missing, but Queen Aleste knew where he was. She was very clever, you know. Prince Ikore was being held captive in a spaceship and Aleste had one of the two keys which opened it. She ran as fast as she could to get to the spaceship, but when she was about two hundred metres away, she saw an army. The army was dressed in a black and brown uniform. It was the same uniform that El Diablo wore. This was El Diablo's surprise for her.

"Oh no, I'll never get past this army unless …" she whispered, "unless I swap clothes with one of them."

Thirty seconds later Aleste was dressed in one of the uniforms. She walked towards the spaceship. Her disguise fooled everyone and she went inside safely. The spaceship was huge. She went into a lot of different rooms before she found the room where Prince Ikore was. Some of the rooms had plasma screens in them, others had windows and some had computers you could only dream of.

Aleste didn't see Ikore at first. Suddenly she heard the sound of snoring. It was Ikore. She followed the sound and found him sleeping behind a computer. She woke him and they started to run like lightning to the exit.

Out of nowhere the ghost of King Jared appeared. He frightened the army waiting outside and guided Ikore and Aleste safely home, where they lived happily for many years.

El Diablo was really angry. He left Mexico and moved to Ireland!

Watch out, he could be living near you!

UNIT 3

Activities

A Fact Finding

1. Aleste was queen of which country?
2. What fell from one of the trees in the queen's garden?
3. Who had El Diablo captured?
4. What was Ikore doing when Aleste entered the spaceship?
5. Who guided Ikore and Aleste safely home?

B Choose the word closest in meaning to the underlined word.

1. Aleste was small and thin, quite the **opposite** of her husband.
   (a) same (b) like
   (c) reverse (d) image
2. She **glanced** up into the tree.
   (a) stared (b) glared
   (c) peeped (d) climbed
3. I have **captured** your only son.
   (a) imprisoned (b) met
   (c) hugged (d) chased after
4. "I'll never get past this army," she **whispered**.
   (a) yelled (b) said quietly
   (c) shouted (d) laughed
5. Her disguise **fooled** everyone.
   (a) pleased (b) surprised
   (c) tricked (d) upset
6. He **guided** Ikore and Aleste safely home.
   (a) walked (b) drove
   (c) followed (d) led

C Choose the most suitable word to complete each sentence.

1. One fine morning Queen Aleste was out ________ with her husband. **(jogging, running, strolling, dancing)**
2. Every time the queen ________ her foot, a pineapple fell. **(lifted, pounded, pointed, touched)**
3. "I'll never get past this army unless I ________ clothes with one of them." **(tear, buy, lose, change)**
4. She walked ________ the spaceship. **(to, past, on, at)**
5. The ghost of King Jared ________ the army waiting outside. **(attacked, scared, fought, captured)**
6. El Diablo was ________ . **(upset, annoyed, livid, sad)**

D

Choose the correct answer.

1. **Queen Aleste had many enemies because**
   (a) she was nasty to people.
   (b) she had stolen money.
   (c) she had stolen sweets.
   (d) she did not have any friends.
2. **What was outside the spaceship?**
   (a) El Diablo's lion.
   (b) El Diablo's ghost.
   (c) El Diablo's army.
   (d) El Diablo's guard dogs.
3. **How did Queen Aleste get inside the spaceship?**
   (a) She became invisible.
   (b) She waited until it was dark.
   (c) She slithered in on the ground.
   (d) She wore a disguise.
4. **What sound did Queen Aleste follow to find Ikore?**
   (a) Snoring.
   (b) Laughter.
   (c) The television.
   (d) Birds singing.
5. **King Jared frightened the army because**
   (a) he was ugly.
   (b) he was a ghost.
   (c) he was an ogre.
   (d) he was bigger than them.

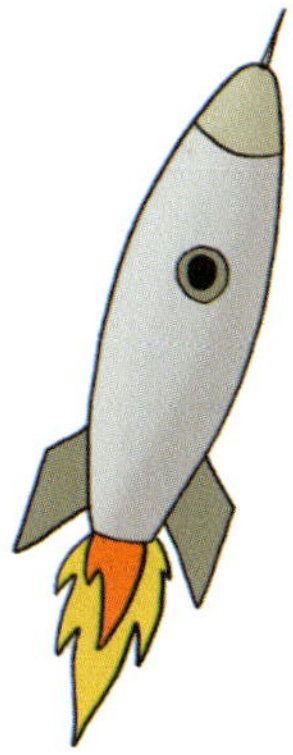

E

Grammar

A question asks something. We put a question mark ? at the end of each question.

Write the questions for these answers.

1. They were walking in the garden.
2. Queen Aleste had blue eyes.
3. El Diablo put poison in King Jared's drink.
4. Two keys opened the spaceship.
5. The army's uniform was black and brown.
6. He moved to Ireland.

F

Explore the Text

This story has a scary feel to it. This feeling is created by different sentences in the story, e.g. "She wasn't a very nice person and had many enemies."

Write the other sentences which help give this story a scary feeling.

G

Character Description

Queen Aleste is the main character in this story. Read the story again and write a description of Aleste in your own words.

DUBLIN ZOO

Home | About the Zoo | Animals and Plants | Visiting the Zoo | News | Learning | Support the Zoo | Shop | Contact

Introduction
Opening Times
Admissions
Meet the Keeper
How to get Here
Zoo Map
Food Outlets

Visiting the Zoo

Discover a World Full of Fun and Adventure!

Introduction

There's a world of animals and a heap of surprises waiting for you at Dublin Zoo.

Come in and spot giraffes and zebras on the Plains of Africa and catch a glimpse of our growing herd of Asian elephants in the Rainforest – and don't worry you can go all round the world and still be home in time for tea.

Visit Dublin Zoo!

There are tigers, hippos, bats, lions, rare monkeys, gorillas, orang-utans, chimpanzees and red pandas to name but a few of the amazing animals you'll find waiting for you around every corner.

There's something for everyone at Dublin Zoo. Look out for keeper talks and animal feeding times. Wander through our stunning grounds and enjoy the colours of the seasons. Dublin Zoo's team of experts take great care to ensure that our animals feel at home – at the same time making our visitors feel they have entered another world.

Adopt-an-Animal

Discover how you can adopt your very own animal!

Find out more!

Become-a-Member

Get great benefits when you become a member of Dublin Zoo!

Get membership today!

DUBLIN ZOO

Home | About the Zoo | Animals and Plants | Visiting the Zoo | News | Learning | Support the Zoo | Shop | Contact

Latest Story

Archived Stories

Zoo Matters

Calendar of Events

News - - - Calendar of Events

March

All About Animals Easter Workshop

A fun event exploring animal habitats and taking a closer look at the weird and wonderful variety of insects living in the Zoo.

Dates: 26th and 27th March

Time: 11am - 3pm

Cost: €16 members, €25 non-members

For children between 6-12 years. To book a place call the Education Department on (01) 4748932 or email: education@dublinzoo.ie

April

Native Species Weekend

If you want to learn more about Ireland's plants and animals, then this is an event you cannot afford to miss. Following on from the success of last year's event, Dublin Zoo and a variety of Irish wildlife groups are hosting another Native Species Weekend.

There will be plenty to keep children (and adults alike) busy with touch-tables, visitors from the sea and hands-on activities! Looking forward to seeing you there!

Dates: 19th and 20th April (no pre-booking required)

May

New – All About Toads & Frogs Workshop

Ever wondered what makes frogs & toads different? Come along and meet our zookeeper who will tell you all you need to know about these wonderful creatures that have been around for over 200 million years! Where do they live? What do they eat?

Dates: 3rd May and 14th June

Time: 11am – 1pm

Cost: €10 members, €25 non-members

For children between 6–12 years. To book a place call the Education Department on (01) 4748932 or email: education@dublinzoo.ie

100% of the fee for this event will go directly towards the Dublin Zoo Amphibian Ark – 'Year of the Frog' campaign.

UNIT 4 Activities

A

Fact Finding

1. Where in the zoo will you spot giraffes and zebras?
2. What will you catch a glimpse of in the Rainforest?
3. Who makes sure that the animals feel at home?
4. In what month is the Native Species Weekend being held?
5. How do you book a place on the All About Toads & Frogs Workshop?

B

Choose the word closest in meaning to the underlined word.

1. **Discover** how you can adopt your very own animal.
   (a) look (b) question
   (c) learn (d) ask
2. Catch a **glimpse** of our growing herd of Asian elephants.
   (a) sight (b) sound
   (c) piece (d) feel
3. **Wander** through our stunning grounds.
   (a) run (b) drive (c) ski (d) walk
4. A fun event **exploring** habitats.
   (a) making (b) painting
   (c) discovering (d) destroying
5. A **variety** of Irish wildlife groups are hosting the workshops.
   (a) herd (b) collection
   (c) pack (d) litter
6. Last year's Native Species weekend was a **success**.
   (a) flop (b) terror
   (c) concert (d) hit

C

Choose the most suitable word to complete each sentence.

1. You can see many ________ animals here. **(ugly, wonderful, small, tame)**
2. Wander through our ________ grounds and enjoy the colours of the seasons. **(beautiful, marshy, boggy, grassy)**
3. In the Easter workshop you can explore animal ________. **(food, needs, groups, homes)**
4. Take a closer look at the ________ and wonderful variety of insects living in Dublin Zoo. **(lovely, normal, pretty, strange)**
5. Irish wildlife groups are ________ another Native Species Weekend. **(leaving, closing, having, ordering)**
6. Our zookeeper will tell you all about these wonderful ________. **(people, colours, toys, beasts)**

D

Choose the correct answer.

1. **The Calendar of Events tells us what is happening**
   (a) each day.
   (b) each hour.
   (c) each month.
   (d) each week.
2. **The workshop in March will teach you all about**
   (a) birds.
   (b) animals.
   (c) people.
   (d) frogs.
3. **Where will there be many hands-on things to do?**
   (a) At the Animals Easter Workshop.
   (b) At the Toads and Frogs Workshop.
   (c) In the Rainforest.
   (d) At the Native Species Weekend.
4. **You will meet the zookeeper if you go to the workshop being held in**
   (a) May.
   (b) February.
   (c) March.
   (d) April.

5. **Frogs and toads are**
   (a) mammals. (b) reptiles.
   (c) amphibians. (d) insects.

E

Grammar

Unscramble these sentences putting in capital letters, full stops and question marks where needed.

1. a heap of there's waiting surprises for you at zoo dublin
2. zoo's experts at home ensure that our dublin animals feel
3. book a education place to on any, call the workshop department
4. toads do and frogs live where and eat
5. growing where you see our herd of asian would elephants
6. the being workshop is held in march easter

F

Summarise

Read the Introduction. Pick out the most important points and rewrite it in your own words.

G

Use Your Imagination

Choose a place of interest near where you live. Design a web page for it.

UNIT 5 Bear and Turtle have a Race

Bear and Turtle were great friends. Everyday they lazed under the trees near the river. They told each other stories and made up tall tales about their adventures. One day Bear told Turtle that he had beaten every animal he had ever raced.

"Ah, but you have never raced against me," said Turtle.

Bear smiled. "Do you think you could win?" he asked.

"Yes!" said Turtle. "We will race tomorrow!"

Before heading for home, the friends planned their race route. They would start near the old cedar tree. They would then run along by the bank of the river, as far as the giant sequoia tree. They placed the finishing marker at this point. They decided to ask Owl to start the race at noon the next day.

On her slow journey home, Turtle started having doubts. She knew she would need a very clever plan to have any chance of winning the race. She gathered all her family around her. They all said they would help. After many hours of talking, they thought of a plan. Each turtle would stand at a different place along the route. The first turtle would stand at the starting point near the old cedar tree. The next would stand near the swamp where Alligator's family lived. The next would stand under the tall oak and the next would stand where Great Blue Heron's nest could be seen. Turtle herself would stand at the giant sequoia, near the finishing marker. She felt very pleased with herself and slept well that night.

The following morning, bright and early, Bear and Turtle met at the starting place near the old cedar. Just before noon Owl arrived. He flew to a branch near the top of the tree. He raised his wing. Bear and Turtle got ready. The race was about to begin!

"Ready, steady, go!" hooted Owl.

Bear took off at an amazing pace. Turtle disappeared into the long grass. When Bear reached the swamp where Alligator lived, he was shocked to see Turtle ahead of him. Bear quickly raced past her, grinning as he went. Along by the river he ran. Bear felt good.

"Turtle will never win," he thought.

But as he followed the bend of the river and came close to the tall oak, he couldn't believe his eyes. There in front of him was Turtle! Bear stepped up the pace and hurried past Turtle again. Turtle chuckled and slowly wandered into the bushes.

When Bear reached Great Blue Heron's nest, Turtle was there before him. Bear was puffing at this stage. He ran as fast as he could, leaving Turtle behind again. Once more Turtle crawled quietly away. Bear, using every bit of strength left in his body, started to sprint. He believed he would now win the race.

Imagine how he felt when he saw Turtle standing at the final marker, beside the giant sequoia tree! Turtle had won the race! Bear could not understand how he had been beaten by a turtle.

Owl flew home with a smile on his face. He had seen it all from the top of the old cedar tree.

UNIT 5 Activities

A Fact Finding

1. What was the race route planned by Bear and Turtle?
2. Why did Turtle gather her family together?
3. When did Owl arrive?
4. What did the first turtle do when the race started?
5. Why was Bear confused?

B Choose the word closest in meaning to the underlined word.

1. Every day Bear and Turtle **lazed** under the trees.
   (a) danced (b) skipped
   (c) stood (d) dozed
2. "Is that a **challenge**?" Bear asked.
   (a) choice (b) chance
   (c) deal (d) dare
3. After many hours of **debate**, a plan was hatched.
   (a) talking (b) eating
   (c) silence (d) thinking
4. Bear took off **at an amazing pace**.
   (a) slowly (b) quietly
   (c) quickly (d) perfectly
5. He was **shocked** to see Turtle ahead of him.
   (a) saddened (b) surprised
   (c) overjoyed (d) happy
6. Bear was **confused**.
   (a) puzzled (b) upset
   (c) delighted (d) furious

C Choose the most suitable word to complete each sentence.

1. They ________ the finishing marker at this point. **(wanted, put, lost, left)**
2. Turtle knew she would need a ________ plan. **(smart, new, different, better)**
3. She felt very ________ with herself. **(annoyed, sad, happy, angry)**
4. Bear took off at a ________ pace. **(slow, wonderful, quick, steady)**
5. Bear stepped up the ________ . **(walk, jog, run, speed)**
6. Turtle ________ quietly away. **(crept, hopped, slid, tiptoed)**

D

Choose the correct answer.

1. **Bear told Turtle that he had**
   (a) eaten every animal he had ever raced.
   (b) beaten every animal he had ever raced.
   (c) fought every animal he had ever raced.
   (d) killed every animal he had ever raced.
2. **When did Turtle and Bear plan to race?**
   (a) That day.
   (b) On Monday.
   (c) The next day.
   (d) At the weekend.
3. **Just before what time did Owl arrive?**
   (a) Midnight.
   (b) Two o'clock.
   (c) Midday.
   (d) Six o'clock.
4. **Bear felt good because**
   (a) he thought he would soon have food.
   (b) he had just eaten honey.
   (c) he had slept well.
   (d) he thought he could win.
5. **Why did Owl have a smile on his face?**
   (a) He was amused at what had happened.
   (b) He was happy to be going home.
   (c) He was shocked by what had happened.
   (d) He was soon going to have his dinner.

E

Grammar

Nouns are naming words, e.g. Bear and Turtle were great fri_'s.

Write these sentences and underline the nouns.

1. They told each other stories and made up tall tales.
2. Turtle knew she would need a clever plan to win the race.
3. Owl flew to the top of the cedar tree.
4. Bear was shocked to see Turtle ahead of him at the swamp.
5. Bear used every bit of strength in his body.
6. Owl flew home with a smile on his face.

F

Summarise

Turtle was afraid she could not win the race. In your own words write the plan Turtle and her family hatched.

G

Use Your Imagination

Owl saw everything from the top of the cedar tree. Imagine you are Owl sitting in your tree house telling your family all about the race.

UNIT 6 Captain Gallant

From *Captain Gallant* by Goldie Alexander (Folens Reading Pack Level 3)

Sometimes, Captain Gallant receives distress calls. To help those in trouble, he heads to a secret cupboard with a spaceship inside.

"Come on!" he calls out to his crew. "We've had a call."

Sned quickly gallops up the spaceship ramp. Clippety-clop. Clippety-clop.

"Where are we going, Captain?" he asks.

Captain Gallant says, "Cozens have invaded Mars. We must rescue the Martians."

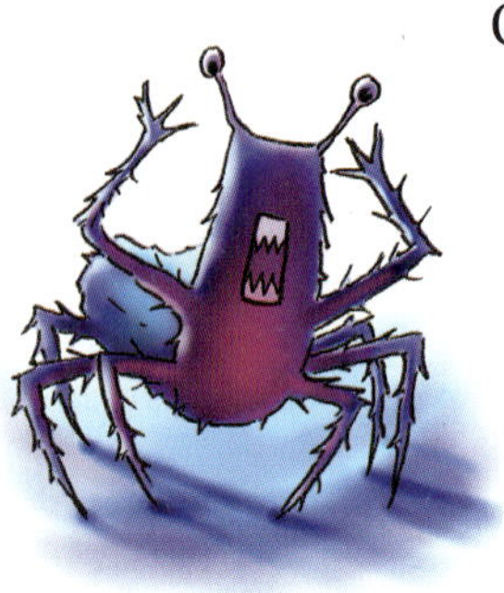

Cozen

Cozens have extra-large eyes, sword-sharp teeth and eight legs covered in hair. Cozens are scary!

Captain Gallant settles in front of the controls. Bork starts the engines. *Venture* picks up speed. Soon, they hover over Mars. Captain Gallant steers *Venture* to a soft landing.

Mars is covered in fine, red dust and there is no air. Before leaving *Venture*, Captain Gallant points to a valley.

"In the centre of that valley is a domed city," he says. "Humans can't live outside that dome."

Sned and Maris

The captain and Ms Megabyte put on their helmets. Then, they head for the city. It has tall buildings and broad streets, but no one is around.

As *Venture*'s crew pass an open doorway, Sned hears a faint cry. He trots inside and returns holding a kitten.

"I think it's sick," he says.

"Not sick, just hungry," Bork growls. Captain Gallant finds a carton of milk inside Ms Megabyte's backpack and feeds the kitten.

"We'll call the kitten Maris," Captain Gallant says. "Maybe she can help us find the Martians."

Maris runs down a flight of stairs. Inside a cellar are the Martian children. Maris races straight into the arms of one of the boys.

“Is this your cat?” asks Captain Gallant.

“Yes,” replies the boy.

“And where are your parents?” the captain asks.

“On the Cozens’ spaceship,” the boy tells him.

“We must rescue them,” says the captain.

“How will you do that?” asks the girl.

“Sned’s strong horns can bend metal and Bork’s breath can weld it together and Ms Megabyte can make herself appear and disappear,” replies Captain Gallant.

“And what can you do?” asks the girl.

Sned says, “Captain Gallant steers *Venture* better than anyone else.”

Ms Megabyte and Captain Gallant

The crew take the children to *Venture*. Halfway to Earth, they come across the Cozens’ spaceship. Its sides bristle with guns. As soon as the Cozens catch sight of *Venture*, they open fire.

Bang! Boom!

A big hole appears in *Venture*’s side. But before all their air can escape, Sned uses his horn to bend the metal into shape. Bork’s fiery breath welds it together. Meanwhile, the Cozens board *Venture*. Everyone is very frightened, but Captain Gallant unlocks his secret cupboard and takes out a giant bottle of Sneezing Mist.

He says, “Ms Megabyte, make yourself invisible and spray the Cozens with this special mist.”

Ms Megabyte sends a misty drizzle through the spaceship. The Cozens start sneezing. Soon, they are sneezing so much they can’t see.

“Hurry!” cries Captain Gallant. “We must board their ship and find the parents.”

The Cozens’ spaceship is dark and scary. Every corner has webs that can trip people up. The crew can’t find the parents anywhere.

Sned says, “Maybe Maris will help us find them. I’ll go and get her.”

Maris leads the crew to the very end of the Cozens’ spaceship. And there are the parents!

UNIT 6

Activities

A

Fact Finding

1. Where does Captain Gallant keep his spaceship?
2. What was the spaceship called?
3. What do Cozens look like?
4. Where is the only place on Mars safe for humans to live?
5. Where did the Martian children hide?

B

Choose the word closest in meaning to the underlined word.

1. Captain Gallant **receives** distress calls.
   (a) hears (b) gets
   (c) likes (d) sends
2. Cozens **invaded** Mars.
   (a) landed on (b) arrived in
   (c) visited (d) attacked
3. The city has **broad** streets.
   (a) narrow (b) stony
   (c) windy (d) wide
4. We must **rescue** the parents.
   (a) save (b) find
   (c) see (d) write to
5. Bork's **fiery** breath welds metal together.
   (a) gentle (b) angry
   (c) harsh (d) flaming
6. Ms Megabyte sent a misty **drizzle** through the spaceship.
   (a) colour (b) smell
   (c) cloud (d) rain

C

Choose the most suitable word to complete each sentence.

1. Soon *Venture* __________ over Mars. **(fluttered, flew, hovered, stopped)**
2. Sned heard a __________ cry. **(loud, distant, quiet, sad)**
3. Bork's breath can __________ metal together. **(push, stick, bend, join)**
4. Sned's strong horns can __________ metal. **(melt, twist, heat, break)**
5. We must __________ the Cozen's ship and find the parents. **(leave, destroy, block, enter)**
6. Maris __________ the crew to the end of the ship. **(guides, drags, pushes, points)**

D Choose the correct answer.

1. **How did Sned become aware of the kitten?**
   (a) He heard a loud sound.
   (b) He heard the kitten mewing.
   (c) He heard the kitten sneezing.
   (d) He heard a faint sound.
2. **Why were the Martian children in the cellar?**
   (a) They were hiding from the Cozens.
   (b) They were playing a game.
   (c) They were keeping dry.
   (d) They were hiding from their parents.
3. **What would happen if the air escaped from *Venture*?**
   (a) Everyone would be upset.
   (b) Everyone would die.
   (c) Everyone would cry.
   (d) Everyone would laugh.
4. **How did Ms Megabyte spray the Cozens without being seen?**
   (a) She was invisible.
   (b) She was clever.
   (c) She wore a disguise.
   (d) She was visible.
5. **Where did the crew find the parents?**
   (a) In the seating.
   (b) In the front of the ship.
   (c) At the back of the ship.
   (d) In the control room.

E Grammar

Write nouns to fill the blanks in these sentences.

1. Captain Gallant's spaceship was in a secret ________ .
2. Very soon the ________ hovers over ________ .
3. The kitten's name is ________ and she drinks ________ .
4. A very large ________ appeared in ________ side.
5. Captain Gallant also had a giant ________ of Sneezing Mist in his ________ .
6. ________ led the ________ to the children's ________ .

F Summarise

In your own words, describe the special powers each crew member has.

G Explore the Text

There are many different types of story, e.g. Horror, Science Fiction, Mystery, Adventure or Funny.

What type of story is "Captain Gallant"? Give some reasons for your answer.

UNIT 7

Talking Animals

Blackberry the horse was tired. His master was a farmer and he made him work very hard. Every day Blackberry worked from early in the morning to late at night. He was allowed one day off a week and he always looked forward to it.

One Saturday night, as the farmer's daughter Anna closed the stable door, she spoke to the horse.

"Rest now, Blackberry," she said. "Tomorrow morning I will bring you out for a run in the near field." The near field was what they called the field nearest the house. "You can graze there all day until the sun goes down. Tomorrow will be a great day of rest for you."

The following morning the farmer awoke.

He said to his daughter, "You must saddle up old Blackberry. I need him to bring me to the market today."

"It is his day off," cried Anna, but she knew she was wasting her time. She walked slowly towards the stable to put the saddle on Blackberry.

When Blackberry saw the girl he whinnied with delight for he really looked forward to his day off. Anna fed the horse and, as she was putting on the saddle, explained that he would have to work that day.

Blackberry was very annoyed.

"Since when do I have to work on Sunday?" he asked.

Anna could not believe her ears. She dropped the saddle in shock and quickly ran back to the house.

"Dad! The horse spoke!" she shouted.

"Don't be a fool," her father said. "Horses don't talk. I'll saddle him up myself."

He marched out of the house towards the barn.

"Dad," Anna called out after him, "Blackberry doesn't want to work today!"

"Whoa! Steady up!" the farmer shouted as he got close to the horse.

He could see that Blackberry was not in a good mood.

"I will not work today. It's my day of rest," said Blackberry, as he lowered his head and stamped his hoof.

The farmer stood back in shock. He dropped the saddle and ran out of the barn.

"I've never heard a horse talk before," he gasped.

"I haven't either," said his dog, Rover.

The farmer bolted back into the house.

"The horse spoke," he told his wife.

"I don't believe you," she cried in shock.

"And when I said that I had never heard a horse speak," the farmer continued, "the dog said he hadn't either."

"That's crazy," said his wife. "Animals can't talk. You go and lie down. I'll saddle up Blackberry and go to market."

"There's nothing crazy about any of that," said the cat, who was lazing on the window ledge. "Have you never heard of a talking horse?"

When the farmer's wife heard this she stumbled towards the nearest armchair and sat down for the rest of the day.

Anna returned to the stable. She was greeted with a whinny and a neigh. Blackberry knew he would not be working that day. He allowed Anna to put on his bridle and lead him to the near field. Once he got there he galloped about with his mane flowing behind him until the sun went down.

The strange thing is that since that day, no one has ever heard Blackberry speak again!

UNIT 7

Activities

A

Fact Finding

1. Who made Blackberry work very hard?
2. Which day of the week was his day off?
3. Where did the farmer want to go?
4. Why did the farmer stand back in shock?
5. Name all the animals who spoke.

B

Choose the word closest in meaning to the underlined word.

1. Blackberry was **allowed** one day off a week.
   (a) promised (b) permitted
   (c) expecting (d) demanding
2. Anna told Blackberry that he could **graze** all day in the field.
   (a) drink (b) run (c) rest (d) feed
3. Blackberry was very **annoyed** that he had to work.
   (a) worried (b) angry
   (c) unhappy (d) sad
4. The farmer **bolted** back into the house.
   (a) ran (b) hopped
   (c) walked (d) strolled
5. The farmer's wife **stumbled** to the nearest armchair.
   (a) sprinted (b) staggered
   (c) crawled (d) jumped
6. Blackberry **galloped** about.
   (a) crawled (b) danced
   (c) walked (d) ran

C

Choose the most suitable word to complete each sentence.

1. The ________ morning, the farmer awoke. **(same, second, next, other)**
2. When Blackberry saw Anna, he ________ with delight. **(smiled, neighed, jumped, strutted)**
3. Anna dropped the saddle in ________. **(awe, fun, surprise, joy)**
4. The farmer could see that Blackberry was in a ________ mood. **(good, happy, jolly, bad)**
5. The farmer's wife thought the farmer was ________. **(asleep, happy, tired, silly)**
6. Blackberry galloped in the near field until ________. **(morning, afternoon, sunset, sunrise)**

D

Choose the correct answer.

1. Blackberry was tired because

(a) he was sick.
(b) he had worked very hard.
(c) he had stayed up late.
(d) he had not slept well.

2. Anna walked slowly towards the stable because

(a) she was frightened.
(b) she was happy.
(c) she was upset.
(d) she was bored.

3. Why was Blackberry annoyed?

(a) He did not like his stable.
(b) He did not like the saddle.
(c) He did not want to work on his day off.
(d) He did not like his oats.

4. The farmer stood back in shock because

(a) Blackberry stamped his hoof
(b) Blackberry refused to work.
(c) Blackberry was annoyed.
(d) Blackberry had spoken.

5. Why did the farmer's wife sit down for the day?

(a) She had got a shock.
(b) She was very tired.
(c) She had a sore foot.
(d) She was watching television.

E

Grammar

Singular means one. Plural means more than one.

Write the plural of the underlined words, e.g. door → doors.

1. Anna closed the stable **door** and spoke to the **horse**.
2. She fed the **animal** and put on his **saddle**.
3. The **farmer** marched out of the **house** towards the **barn**.
4. "It is my **day** of rest," he said as he lowered his **head**.
5. The **cat** was lazing on the window **ledge**.
6. The **horse** galloped in the **field** with his **mane** flowing behind him.

F

Character Description

Blackberry was determined not to work on Sunday.

This tells us a little about Blackberry's personality. Can you think of three more words that would describe Blackberry's personality?

G

Use Your Imagination

Blackberry was tired because he worked hard all week. Pretend you are Blackberry. Cat and Rover the dog visit you in your stable one evening. You are very tired. Tell them all about the work the farmer makes you do.

UNIT 8 Skate Special

From *An Interview with Cindy Centipede* by Goldie Alexander
(Folens Reading Pack Level 3)

Recently, Skate Special had the pleasure of talking to champion in-line skater, Cindy Centipede.

Skate Special

Can you start by telling us a bit about skating?

Cindy Centipede

For many years, skating has been a sport that many people enjoy. Some people skate on concrete and wood, wearing skates with wheels on them. Some skates have blades that can move on ice.

There are many skating sports such as ice hockey and figure skating, but some people like to skate just for fun.

Skate Special

What exactly is in-line skating?

Cindy Centipede

In-line skating is like ice skating, but in-line skaters don't skate on ice. In-line skates have four wheels instead of a blade.

Skate Special

Who invented in-line skates?

Cindy Centipede

The first in-line skates were developed over 300 years ago by a Dutchman who wanted to ice-skate in summer. He nailed wooden reels to strips of wood and fixed them to his boots. These skates were called skeelers, which is the Dutch name for skates.

Diagram of an In-line Skate

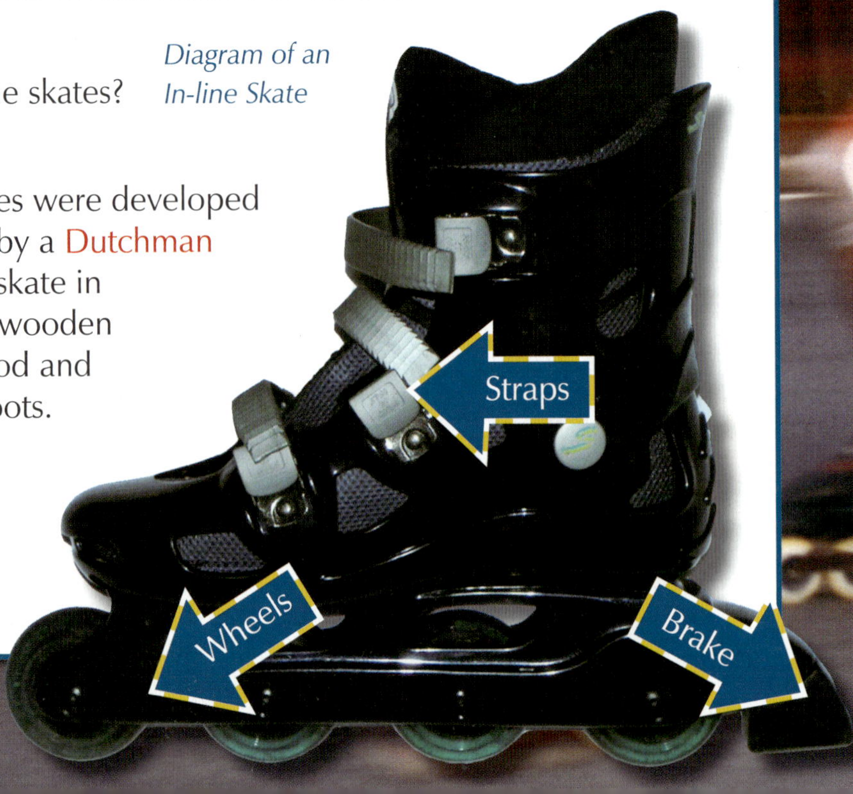

In 1863, James Plimpton made a four-wheel skate with two pairs of wheels side by side. These skates were known as quad skates. Then in 1980, Scott and Brennan Olsen, both ice-hockey players, invented the modern in-line skate. They changed the wheels so they could practise skating the same way as they did on ice. They also added a rubber brake at the back of each skate.

Skate Special

What else do beginners need to know?

Cindy Centipede

Beginners need to know basic turning. To turn you need to practise skating on the curved sides of the skate wheels. This is known as edging. It is also good to learn to bring your feet in and out to make an hourglass figure or a figure of eight. This helps you learn how to control your skates.

Another thing you might like to try is to pretend that you are marching on your in-line skates. When you march on your skates it makes you keep your body straight and your feet underneath you and not out to the side of your body. This will stop you from falling and hurting yourself.

In-line Skating Rules

Rule 1:
Always wear safety gear. This will stop you from getting hurt.

Rule 2:
Know how to turn, how to control your speed, and how to stop.

Rule 3:
Stay away from places where there are a lot of people and cars.

Rule 4:
Watch out for uneven ground. You can easily fall over and hurt yourself.

Rule 5:
If you are skating on the footpath, you have to give way to people who are walking.

Rule 6:
Do not skate in the rain. Rain can rust your skates. Then they will not work and they will be unsafe.

Rule 7:
Wear bright clothes and bright tape if you are skating where the light is not good, so that other people can see you.

UNIT 8

Activities

A

Fact Finding

1. Name some skating sports.
2. What are the differences between in-line skating and ice skating?
3. Who developed the first in-line skates?
4. What helps you learn to control your skates?
5. What must you do if you are skating on footpaths?

B

Choose the word closest in meaning to the underlined word.

1. **Recently**, Skate Special talked to Cindy Centipede.
   (a) suddenly (b) carefully
   (c) possibly (d) lately
2. Who **invented** in-line skates?
   (a) drew (b) created
   (c) photographed (d) sold
3. Scott and Brennan Olsen invented the **modern** in-line skate.
   (a) old (b) stale
   (c) first (d) up-to-date
4. You should know **basic** turning.
   (a) simple (b) difficult
   (c) tricky (d) risky
5. This helps you learn how to **control** your skates.
   (a) check (b) manage
   (c) use (d) clean
6. It makes you keep your feet **underneath** you.
   (a) above (b) beneath
   (c) beside (d) over

C

Choose the most suitable word to complete each sentence.

1. Cindy Centipede is a ________ in-line skater. **(new, poor, novice, prize-winning)**
2. He nailed wooden reels to strips of wood and ________ them to his boots. **(attached, hammered, sewed, showed)**
3. We can see the brake, straps and wheels in the ________ of the in-line skate. **(photograph, painting, drawing, diary)**
4. They changed the wheels so they could ________ the same way they did on ice. **(train, drive, ski, slide)**
5. Learn to make an hourglass ________ . **(picture, shape, number, person)**
6. Always wear safety ________ . **(skates, outfits, equipment, tools)**

D

Choose the correct answer.

1. What did the Dutchman fix onto his boots?

(a) Wooden reels.
(b) Strips of wood.
(c) Strips of wood nailed to wooden reels.
(d) Wooden reels nailed to strips of wood.

2. What were the skates invented by James Plimpton called?

(a) Uni-skates.
(b) Bi-skates.
(c) Quad skates.
(d) Quin skates.

3. In-line skaters

(a) always skate on ice.
(b) do not skate on ice.
(c) do not skate on concrete.
(d) do not skate on wood.

4. You are edging when you

(a) skate on the back of your wheels.
(b) skate on the straight edge of your skate.
(c) skate on the curved sides of the wheels.
(d) skate on the front of the wheels.

5. Wear bright clothes when skating in dim light so you can be

(a) seen.
(b) heard.
(c) faster.
(d) famous.

E

Grammar

Add es to write the plural of words ending in sh, ch, x and s, e.g. fox → foxes.

Write the plural of the underlined words.

1. In **competition**, Cindy **Centipede** skates in the top **class**.
2. This **interview** was done by Freddie **Fox**.
3. Cindy's biggest **wish** was to be a **champion** in-line **skater**.
4. It is good to practise a **march** on your in-line skates.
5. Watch out for the uneven **path**. You could fall and get a serious **scratch**.
6. Store your **skate** and **helmet** in a large **box**.

F

Summarise

Skate Special asked Cindy Centipede what beginners need to know. Write a summary of her answer.

G

Use Your Imagination

This piece is an interview. Imagine you are a reporter. Read the story in Unit 6 again. Write the interview you have done with Captain Gallant talking to him about his recent journey to Mars.

UNIT 9 The Wizards' Contest

It was decided that a contest would be held to find the greatest wizard in the world. Wizards gathered in different towns and villages in countries all over the world to see who was the most talented wizard. Finally, after a number of rounds, there were four wizards left in the contest. These four wizards were invited to compete against each other. The winner would be the world's greatest wizard.

The four wizards spent a year travelling far and wide to gather new spells and perfect their skills. They then met in a faraway village for the Wizards' Contest.

The youngest wizard, whose name was Dal, felt very nervous. The other wizards were much older than him. He knew he could only do his best but wasn't sure that would be enough! Finally the contest began.

The first Wizard, dressed in splendid purple robes, stepped forward.

"Look at what I can do!" he shouted. He raised his wand and before him appeared a small bottle full of yellow liquid.

"What is this?" the other wizards asked.

"Wait and see," he answered.

Guided by the wizard's wand, the bottle slowly turned on its side. As the liquid poured onto the ground, it changed shape and took the form of a lion's head and a lion's tail.

"That's nothing!" said the second wizard. "My magic is much greater."

He pointed his wand at the head and tail of the lion. There was a flash of light and the lion's body became complete.

The second wizard was very quickly followed by the third.

"Ah, but the animal does not move," the third wizard said. "Now you shall see the greatest magic of all!"

He twirled his wand, shouted some magic words and within seconds the lion's tail began to tremble. Then its eyelids began to flutter. Before long its eyes were open.

The wizards were all silent. In all their travels they had not seen such amazing magic. To be able to bring an animal as dangerous as a lion to life with one flick of your wand was truly powerful magic. They waited to see what the fourth wizard could do!

Dal had watched in silence. He had seen a lion conjured up from a yellow liquid and had now seen the animal come to life.

"I cannot match your magic," he said. "I have only learned simple tricks from simple magicians."

"You must try!" the others said. "Believe in yourself!"

While the wizards were talking, they had not noticed that the lion had turned his attention towards them. He opened his huge mouth, roared loudly and pounced. Dal thought quickly. He stamped his feet twice and in a flash a cage appeared, trapping the lion.

The other three wizards all turned towards Dal.

"You have just saved our lives," the second wizard said.

"I put our lives at risk," said the third wizard.

The first wizard spoke. "Great magic must always be used with care and concern for others. It is the first rule you learn when you train to be a wizard. We forgot it, because we were trying to prove how great we were. But you did not forget! If you had not been here to work your most powerful magic, we would be dead."

The wizards agreed that Dal was indeed the greatest and wisest wizard in the world.

UNIT 9

Activities

A Fact Finding

1. How many wizards were invited to compete in the contest?
2. How long did they spend travelling?
3. Why did Dal feel nervous?
4. What happened to the liquid when it poured onto the ground?
5. Who won the Wizards' Contest?

B Choose the word closest in meaning to the underlined word.

1. A contest was held to find the **greatest** wizard in the world.
   (a) biggest (b) nicest
   (c) most powerful (d) most fun
2. They spent a year **travelling**.
   (a) walking (b) flying
   (c) sailing (d) journeying
3. The wizard wore **splendid** robes.
   (a) beautiful (b) nice
   (c) pretty (d) awful
4. "Wait and see," he **answered**.
   (a) sang (b) shouted
   (c) thought (d) replied
5. The liquid took the **shape** of a lion's head and a lion's tail.
   (a) picture (b) form
   (c) video (d) body
6. He **twirled** his wand.
   (a) spun (b) dropped
   (c) lifted (d) shook

C Choose the most suitable word to complete each sentence.

1. The lion's tail began to ________ . **(jump, shake, shrink, grow)**
2. He had seen a lion ________ up from a yellow liquid. **(summoned, lifted, raised, swung)**
3. The lion turned his ________ towards the wizards. **(head, eyes, face, interest)**
4. "I put our lives ________ ," said the third wizard. **(in safety, in danger, in motion, in chaos)**
5. Great magic must be used with care and ________ for others. **(happiness, joy, regard, disregard)**
6. The wizards were trying to ________ how great they were. **(show, believe, correct, destroy)**

D

Choose the correct answer.

1. Why were there only four wizards left to compete?

(a) No one else was interested.

(b) They had got to the final.

(c) There were no other wizards.

(d) They asked to be let compete.

2. The four wizards spent a year travelling to

(a) practise their magic.

(b) see new countries.

(c) improve their magic.

(d) teach new tricks.

3. What did the third wizard think was the greatest magic of all?

(a) To bring an animal to life.

(b) To send an animal to sleep.

(c) To make an animal talk.

(d) To talk to an animal.

4. Dal believed he could not match the other wizards' magic

(a) because he was shy.

(b) because he was young.

(c) because he was afraid.

(d) because he was insecure.

5. Dal became the greatest wizard in the world because

(a) he had saved the others.

(b) he had concern for others.

(c) he knew the rules.

(d) he knew more magic.

E

Grammar

Comparing words: Rich – Richer – Richest

Choose the correct word to finish the sentence.

1. A contest was held to find the ________ wizard in the world. **(greater, greatest)**
2. All the other wizards were ________ than Dal. **(older, oldest)**
3. Dal was the ________ wizard. **(younger, youngest)**
4. The second wizard shouted ________ than the first. **(louder, loudest)**
5. The third wizard thought he was the ________ . **(smarter, smartest)**
6. Dal became known as the ________ wizard in the world. **(wiser, wisest)**

F

Character Description

At the end of this story Dal is described as the wisest wizard in the world. Write a short piece describing Dal's character.

G

Use Your Imagination

Imagine you are the lion in this story. Write about what happened in your own words. Remember to include what happened to you after Dal won the contest.

UNIT 10

A Hairy Story

From *A Hairy Story* by Goldie Alexander
(Folens Reading Pack Level 3)

"Three wishes!" said Ben.

He didn't mind three wishes, but he didn't believe what the old man said at all.

The old man leaned back in his chair and smiled.

"So what is your first wish?" he asked.

Ben stared at himself in the mirror again. Oh, how he hated this new haircut.

"I wish," he said as loud as he could, "I wish my hair would grow again really fast."

"No sooner said than done," said the old man, his eyes twinkling like stars on a dark night.

And right then, Ben's hair started to grow. And GROW and GROW … until it was halfway down his back.

"That's enough!" shouted Ben.

But Ben's hair took no notice. It was out of control. Soon, it was long enough to reach the ground. Instead of stopping there, the hair snaked across the hairdresser's floor. It curled around the hairdresser's legs. It curled over all the people sitting in chairs waiting to have their hair cut. It covered the magazines so no one could read them. It curled along the washbasins and twisted around the taps. It curled along the mirrors so the startled faces looked as though they had put on curly, ginger wigs. It curled around the lights so the room got dark and the hairdresser couldn't see what he was doing.

The hairdresser was really mad.

"Stop that hair growing!" he yelled. "Or I could cut someone's ear off by mistake!"

But Ben didn't know how to stop his hair. It was totally out of control.

"That's enough!" he yelled again.

Again, his hair took no notice. It just kept on growing until it reached the door. It curled its way outside. It curled around a parking meter and a streetlight. Next, it coiled around a cyclist and went right over a passing car.

The people were mad.

"Stop that hair growing!" they yelled.

But Ben's hair took no notice. It stopped all the traffic and slid into any open car window it could find. It even twisted its way around a police officer who came to sort things out!

"Stop that hair growing!" everyone yelled.

But no one could do anything to control Ben's hair. Soon, it was so thick and long that nothing could get through at all. Trucks, buses and cars were banked up everywhere. It was one gigantic traffic jam!

Then Ben's hair started to wind up into the air. It grew and grew and grew. Soon, it wound around a truck, then a bus, then a bridge, then a skyscraper and then a plane.

The pilot of the plane was really annoyed! He called the airport and told them to send all the other planes to another airport.

Everything had come to a stop. No one and nothing could move. Not even Ben. His hair had him trapped in his chair.

"Stop, stop!" he yelled over and over. "I wish my hair would stop growing!"

"No sooner said than done," said the old man with twinkling eyes, and Ben's hair stopped growing.

UNIT 10

Activities

A Fact Finding

1. How many wishes did Ben have?
2. What happened when Ben's hair curled around the lights?
3. What did Ben's hair do when it reached the door?
4. What did the pilot of the plane do?
5. What was Ben's second wish?

B Choose the word closest in meaning to the underlined word.

1. The old man **leaned** back.
   (a) twisted (b) tilted
   (c) turned (d) toppled
2. Right then, Ben's hair **started** to grow.
   (a) decided (b) began
   (c) wanted (d) wished
3. The hair **snaked** across the hairdresser's floor.
   (a) danced (b) flew
   (c) ran (d) twisted
4. The **startled** faces looked as though they had put on wigs.
   (a) shocked (b) happy
   (c) annoyed (d) pretty
5. The hairdresser was really **mad**.
   (a) pale (b) boring
   (c) angry (d) pleased
6. Ben's hair **coiled** around a cyclist.
   (a) curled (b) danced
   (c) zig-zagged (d) jogged

C Choose the most suitable word to complete each sentence.

1. Ben ________ everything that the old man said. **(believed, accepted, doubted, forgot)**
2. The old man's eyes were ________ like stars on a dark night. **(shining, flashing, pretty, bright)**
3. The hairdresser was afraid he might cut off someone's ear ________. **(on purpose, in fear, by accident, by chance)**
4. "Stop that hair growing," the people ________. **(asked, said, whispered, screamed)**
5. No one could ________ Ben's hair. **(manage, cut, style, catch)**
6. In the end there was one ________ traffic jam. **(big, enormous, large, great)**

D

Choose the correct answer.

1. **Where was Ben when he met the old man?**
   (a) In school.
   (b) In the shop.
   (c) In the hairdresser's.
   (d) In the library.
2. **Ben wanted his hair to grow really fast because**
   (a) he liked long hair.
   (b) he did not like his new haircut.
   (c) he wanted a ponytail.
   (d) he did not want to wear a hat.
3. **What colour was Ben's hair?**
   (a) Brown. (b) Blonde.
   (c) Black. (d) Ginger.
4. **What was the police officer trying to do?**
   (a) Direct traffic.
   (b) Sort things out.
   (c) Check for road tax.
   (d) Cross the road.
5. **Why was Ben unable to move?**
   (a) His hair had tied him to the chair.
   (b) He was very tired.
   (c) He had a broken leg.
   (d) He had frozen in fear.

E

Grammar

Four, one, six, two. These numbers are in Alphabetical Order.

Write the following words in alphabetical order.

1. Washbasin, scissors, taps, mirror
2. Twisted, coiled, snaked, wound
3. Hair, face, nose, mouth
4. Truck, bus, car, plane
5. Yell, roar, shout, bellow, call
6. Pilot, astronaut, driver, cyclist, sailor

F

Explore the Text

The tone of "Queen Aleste saves Prince Ikore" was scary. What is the tone of this story? (Funny, scary, sad, etc.) Find three sentences in the story which help set the tone.

G

Use Your Imagination

Ben had three wishes. In this extract he only used two of them. How do you think this story ends? What might Ben's third wish have been?

UNIT 11

Brave Hans

Hans lived in a city in Holland called Haarlem. He was a young boy who loved helping his mother and father. One afternoon Hans's mother was baking cakes. She asked Hans to bring some cakes to an old man who lived in the country. The man was blind and lived by himself. Hans's parents often visited him and brought him food.

"Don't delay, Hans," his mother warned. "It is autumn and it gets dark early."

The old man was delighted with the gift. Hans chatted with him for a short while but then explained that he had to go straight home. He said goodbye and started on the long walk home.

Haarlem, like many other cities in Holland, was built on land which had been reclaimed from the sea. In many places the land was lower than the sea and the people built strong walls to keep the water out. Everyone in Haarlem knew that if anything happened to those walls, the whole countryside would be flooded. As he walked home, Hans noticed that the water was quite high. This was because there had been a lot of rain.

Hans decided to gather some wild flowers for his mother. Then he picked some seed heads. He blew the heads and watched the seeds float high up into the air. Along the way, he noticed a family of rabbits playing happily in the grass. He remembered the smile that had been on the old man's face when he had given him the cakes.

Hans suddenly realised that it was getting late. He was starting to feel hungry and his belly was rumbling. He remembered his mother's warning not to delay. To his dismay, he noticed that it was beginning to get dark and he was still a good distance away from home. He started to walk faster and then he decided to run.

Suddenly he stopped. He thought he heard a sound like water dripping.

"It couldn't be water," he thought.

He looked around and could not believe his eyes. There was a small hole in the wall and a steady stream of water was trickling through it. Hans knew that the hole had to be blocked! He started to panic.

"Help! Help!" he shouted, but nobody heard him.

Hans did the only thing he could. He stuck his finger in the hole to keep the water out. Now all he had to do was wait until someone passed by.

As darkness fell, Hans felt very scared. He kept shouting but no one came to his aid. Just as he had given up hope of being rescued before morning, Hans heard voices calling his name.

"Hans, Hans, where are you?"

Hans drew in a deep breath and shouted as loudly as he could, "I'm here! Help me!"

He heard his parents' voices and the sound of footsteps running towards him.

"We're coming, Hans!" they shouted.

Within minutes his mother was beside him.

"There's a hole in the wall," Hans cried, "and I didn't know what else to do!"

The people in the search party were shocked. They set to work making the wall stronger.

Hans was wrapped in a blanket and brought safely home. He was very, very tired.

"I kept the sea out," he said to his mother.

"Yes, brave Hans," his mother replied, "You are a hero, you saved our city from flooding."

UNIT 11

Activities

A

Fact Finding

1. In which country would you find the city of Haarlem?
2. What could happen if the walls around Haarlem were damaged?
3. What did Hans do when he realised it was getting late?
4. How did Hans react when he saw the water trickling through the hole?
5. Who rescued Hans?

B

Choose the word closest in meaning to the underlined word.

1. The old man **was blind**.
   (a) could not see (b) could not hear
   (c) could not speak
   (d) could not walk
2. He was **delighted** with his gift.
   (a) amazed (b) surprised
   (c) thrilled (d) offended
3. The land had been **reclaimed** from the sea.
   (a) stolen (b) washed up
   (c) sent (d) recovered
4. His belly was **rumbling**.
   (a) sore (b) growling
   (c) fat (d) sick
5. He remembered his mother's warning not to **delay**.
   (a) hurry (b) run
   (c) linger (d) leave
6. A steady stream of water was **trickling** through the hole.
   (a) gushing (b) flooding
   (c) rushing (d) dripping

C

Choose the most suitable word to complete each sentence.

1. Hans ________ the old man's smile. **(realised, recalled, painted, forgot)**
2. A ________ stream of water trickled through the hole in the wall. **(fast, rushing, non-stop, rapid)**
3. Hans kept shouting, but no one came to his ________. **(mind, help, attention, place)**
4. Hans had nearly given up hope of being ________ before morning. **(seen, awake, dry, saved)**
5. The people in the search party were ________. **(defeated, thrilled, stunned, elated)**
6. Hans was ________ in a blanket and brought safely home. **(hidden, covered, dried, tied)**

D Choose the correct answer.

1. **Why did Hans's mother tell him not to delay?**
   (a) He still had his chores to do.
   (b) She wanted him home before dark.
   (c) She wanted him to bring cakes to other people.
   (d) She wanted him home before the river started flooding.
2. **Why were strong walls built around Haarlem?**
   (a) To keep the water warm.
   (b) To keep the water clean.
   (c) To keep the water in.
   (d) To keep the water out.
3. **Why did the hole have to be blocked?**
   (a) Because the water would have soaked Hans's feet.
   (b) Because the water would have drowned the flowers.
   (c) Because the water would have flooded the city.
   (d) Because the water was cold.
4. **How did Hans get the attention of the search party?**
   (a) He shouted loudly.
   (b) He threw stones in the water.
   (c) He sent up a flare.
   (d) He lit a fire.

5. **What did Hans's parents do when he did not come home?**
   (a) They cried.
   (b) They organized a party.
   (c) They rang the police.
   (d) They organized a search party.

E Grammar

Lazed, lived, loved, lulled. These words are written in Alphabetical Order.

Write the following words in alphabetical order. Underline the second letter of each word before you start.

1. Country, city, canal, current
2. Fear, fright, faint, float
3. Rumble, remember, rabbits, roll
4. Delay, dismay, darkness, dripping,
5. Hans, hero, Holland, higher, hug
6. Bake, brave, block, belly, boy

F Summarise

Hans started to panic when he saw the hole in the wall. Read the paragraphs which describe what he did and how he felt while he waited to be rescued. Rewrite these paragraphs in not more than five lines.

G Use Your Imagination

You are a reporter for *The Daily Blurb*. You have been sent to Hans's home to interview him about what had happened. Give yourself a name and write the article.

UNIT 12

Jakub and the Kaha Bird

Jakub was a fisherman. He was sad because he was too old to travel on the trawlers and fish at sea. He decided that he would only fish in the river.

Every morning Jakub rose early. He went to the river, sat on a rock and cast out his line. Then he waited for the fish to bite. There was a market in the village where Jakub lived and every evening he went there to sell whatever fish he had caught. There were very few fish in the river. Jakub was earning very little money.

One hot day, Jakub was sitting in his usual spot feeling very weary. Suddenly he noticed a beautiful silver bird standing on the rock beside him. He could not believe his eyes. It was the Kaha bird! The Kaha bird was a very rare bird. People believed that it brought good fortune to anybody who saw it.

"You look sad. Have you no one to care for you?" asked the Kaha bird.

"No," replied Jakub. "I am tired because I fish from early morning to late at night and earn very little money for food."

"You are too old to have to work so hard," the Kaha bird said. "From now on I will care for you. I will leave a large fish on your doorstep every day. Do with it what you will."

That evening the fisherman returned home happy.

True to her word, the very next evening, the bird left a large fish on Jakub's doorstep. He brought it to the market, sold it and got a lot of money in return. This happened every day. Soon Jakub was a very rich man.

One evening as he left the market, Jakub overheard a group of people talking.

"The king has heard of a great bird called the Kaha bird. If anyone can help him capture it, he will reward that person well," they said.

Jakub joined the crowd and asked if anyone knew why the king wanted the Kaha bird.

One man replied, "The king is losing his sight. A wise, old man has told him that he will regain his sight if a Kaha bird is killed. The king has promised half his kingdom and half his wealth as a reward to anyone who can help him capture the bird."

The old fisherman had become greedy. He went to the king and told him that he could help him capture the bird. The king was very pleased and ordered his soldiers to go to the old man's house that evening. They hid in Jakub's house and waited.

When the Kaha arrived with the fish, Jakub was there to greet her. He invited her into his house.

"I have never thanked you," he said, "please come inside. I have prepared a feast for us to share."

The Kaha slowly flew down and landed on a rock near where Jakub stood. As she did so, the king's soldiers rushed out and tried to grab her. Jakub knew that he could lose everything if the bird escaped. He ran to help the soldiers. He held on to one of the great bird's legs.

The Kaha flapped her powerful wings and started to rise high in the sky with Jakub still holding on to her leg. The Kaha spread those mighty wings and soared higher. Soon Jakub and the Kaha were just dots in the sky. They were never seen again.

UNIT 12

Activities

A Fact Finding

1. Where did Jakub sell his fish?
2. What colour is the Kaha bird?
3. What did people believe would happen if you saw the Kaha bird?
4. How did the Kaha bird help Jakub?
5. Why did the king want to capture the Kaha bird?

B Choose the word closest in meaning to the underlined word.

1. He was **earning** very little money.
   (a) spending (b) losing
   (c) making (d) saving
2. Jakub was feeling very **weary**.
   (a) tired (b) cross
   (c) unwell (d) sad
3. That evening the fisherman **returned** home happy.
   (a) slithered
   (b) left
   (c) arrived
   (d) wiggled
4. The king will **regain** his sight if a Kaha bird is killed.
   (a) lose (b) keep
   (c) retain (d) recover
5. The king has promised half his **wealth** as a reward.
   (a) palace (b) riches
   (c) land (d) food
6. The Kaha bird spread those mighty wings and **soared** higher.
   (a) looked (b) flew
   (c) flapped (d) wobbled

C Choose the most suitable word to complete each sentence.

1. He ________ out his fishing line. **(put, threw, dropped, handed)**
2. The king has ________ to give half his kingdom as a reward. **(agreed, wanted, begged, begun)**
3. The old man had become ________ . **(angry, ill, mean, kind)**
4. Jakub ________ the Kaha bird into his house. **(pushed, forced, locked, asked)**
5. "I have ________ a feast for us to share," Jakub said. **(bought, ordered, burnt, arranged)**
6. The soldiers tried to ________ the bird. **(trip, grasp, tackle, tease)**

D

Choose the correct answer.

1. Why was Jakub weary?

(a) He had been up late.

(b) He had not slept well.

(c) He was working hard and earning very little money.

(d) He was ill.

2. How did Jakub become rich?

(a) He won the lottery.

(b) He sold a large fish in the market each day.

(c) He found gold at the end of the rainbow.

(d) He was given a reward.

3. Where did Jakub overhear the people talking?

(a) At the shop.

(b) At the palace.

(c) At the market place.

(d) At his home.

4. Who told the king he could regain his sight if a Kaha bird was killed?

(a) A wise, old man.

(b) The queen.

(c) Jakub.

(d) A soldier.

5. How did Jakub try to help the soldiers catch the bird?

(a) He held on to one of her wings.

(b) He held on to one of her feathers.

(c) He held on to her beak.

(d) He held on to one of her legs.

E

Grammar

Rewrite these sentences putting in the capital letters.

1. every monday morning jakub rose early.
2. jakub could no longer fish from his trawler, the marie-rose.
3. he travelled to the market in roseville on easter sunday.
4. "i will reward the person who captures the kaha bird," king john said.
5. king john ordered tom, fred and mick to go to the man's house.
6. the kaha bird brought jakub to mars.

F

Summarise

Jakub decided to help the king capture the Kaha bird. In your own words, tell how he tried to do this.

G

Character Description

"You are too old to work so hard," the Kaha bird said. "From now on I will care for you." This tells us about the bird's character. What words would you use to describe the Kaha bird?

UNIT 13

"Moko" to the Rescue!

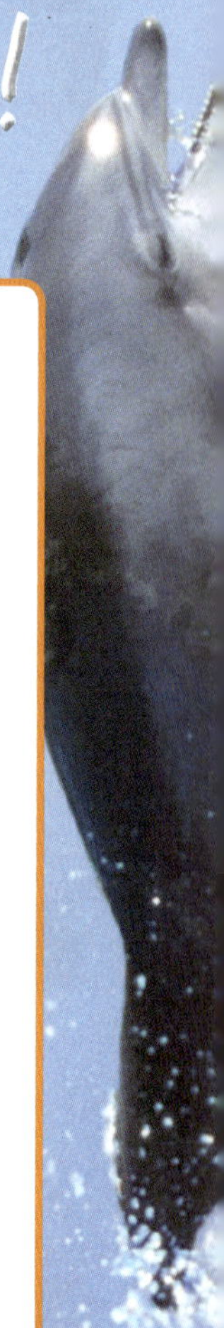

In March 2008, a dolphin came to the rescue of two very distressed whales who were stranded on a beach in New Zealand. Local people called the dolphin "Moko".

Two pygmy sperm whales, a mother and her calf, were found stranded on Mahia beach about three hundred miles from New Zealand's capital city, Wellington. Rescuers were called in to help free the whales. They worked for more than an hour trying to get them back into the water and safely out to sea. However each time the whales moved, they became stranded again on a sand bar which was in the sea, slightly out from the beach. The sand bar was blocking their way to deeper water. This happened many times and rescuers were beginning to despair for the safety of the whales, who were becoming more and more confused.

Then suddenly, to the amazement of the would-be rescuers, a beautiful bottle-nosed dolphin came flying through the water, pushed between them and approached the whales. By this stage the whales were arching their backs and calling to one another. As if by magic, however, they suddenly seemed to relax. They submerged themselves in the water and allowed themselves be led by Moko through a channel and safely out to sea.

Malcolm Smith, one of the rescue workers, said the rescue group were about to give up on the rescue when Moko appeared.

"The whales were tired and we were all cold. We were beginning to give up hope of saving them and then Moko arrived. We heard Moko and the whales make noises and then it was as if she took them by their flippers and led them to safety. It was incredible to see," Mr Smith said.

"Rescued whales often return to the place where they were stranded," Mr Smith added. "But it seems that Moko brought these whales far out of the area because we haven't seen them since. She really is an amazing dolphin!"

Bottle-nosed dolphins are very friendly dolphins and are known to be very caring creatures.

Mark Simmonds, whose work is to protect whales and dolphins, said, "Dolphins are able to plan and think ahead and can coax other creatures to follow them. They would not have understood what the whales were saying but would have sensed that they were in danger. They are known to swim with different species of whale so it would not be unusual for these creatures to 'talk' to each other."

Moko seems to have been separated from her pod and has made Mahia beach her home. For the last few months she has been playing in the surf with swimmers and pushing kayaks through the water with her snout.

After the rescue, Moko returned to the beach and spent the rest of the day playing in the water with local people.

This report has been taken from an article published in *The Times* on 13th March 2008.

UNIT 13

Activities

A Fact Finding

1. Where were the two whales stranded?
2. What was blocking their way to deeper water?
3. What type of dolphin was Moko?
4. Who was about to give up on the rescue when Moko appeared?
5. Where did Moko return to after the rescue?

B Choose the word closest in meaning to the underlined word.

1. Two pygmy sperm whales were found **stranded** on Mahia beach.
   (a) playing (b) stuck
   (c) chatting (d) surfing
2. The whales were becoming more and more **confused**.
   (a) confident (b) excited
   (c) playful (d) bewildered
3. They suddenly seemed to relax and **submerge** in the water.
   (a) sink (b) dive (c) swim (d) lie
4. It was **incredible** to see.
   (a) horrible (b) lovely
   (c) unbelievable (d) usual
5. Mark Simmonds's job is to **protect** whales and dolphins.
   (a) endanger (b) preserve
   (c) attack (d) count
6. Moko had been pushing **kayaks** through the water.
   (a) canoes (b) liners
   (c) trawlers (d) ships

C Choose the most suitable word to complete each sentence.

1. The sand bar ________ the way out. (**showed, barred, marked, lit**)
2. To the ________ of would-be rescuers, a bottle-nosed dolphin came flying through the water. (**surprise, upset, annoyance, anger**)
3. Rescued whales often ________ the place where they were stranded. (**destroy, love, remember, revisit**)
4. Dolphins can ________ other creatures to follow them. (**order, persuade, force, push**)
5. Dolphins are known to swim with different ________ of whales. (**families, colours, types, ages**)
6. It would not be ________ for whales and dolphins to "talk" to each other. (**usual, normal, strange, useful**)

D

Choose the correct answer.

1. **What type of whales were stranded on the beach?**
   (a) Humpback whales.
   (b) Killer whales.
   (c) Pygmy sperm whales.
   (d) Blue whales.
2. **Rescuers were called in to help**
   (a) paint the whales.
   (b) save the whales.
   (c) capture the whales.
   (d) catch the whales.
3. **The rescuers could see the whales were upset because they were**
   (a) arching their fins.
   (b) arching their eyebrows.
   (c) arching their necks.
   (d) arching their backs.
4. **Where was the sand bar?**
   (a) Far out to sea.
   (b) Far out from the beach.
   (c) Close to the beach.
   (d) In the distance.
5. **What did Moko do after the rescue?**
   (a) She returned to the beach.
   (b) She returned to the sand bar.
   (c) She returned to the whales.
   (d) She returned to her pod.

E

Grammar

Sometimes you add s to write the plural of words ending in o and sometimes you add es, e.g. video → videos, hero → heroes.

Write the singular of the underlined words.

1. The **dolphins** were local **heroes**.
2. The **onlookers** made **videos** of the **rescues**.
3. In the **photos**, **cuckoos** could be seen flying overhead.
4. The **rescuers** were able to hear the **echoes** of the **noises**.
5. Luckily, there were no **tornadoes** on the **beaches**.

F

Explore the Text

"Moko to the Rescue" is a newspaper article. Articles need to start with a good headline, stick to the facts, include interviews and give general information if necessary.

Read the article again and find one example of each of these.

G

Use Your Imagination

Read the story "Brave Hans" again. It is in Unit 11.

Write a newspaper article about how Hans saved the city.

UNIT 14

The Magic Horse

From *The Magic Horse* by Edel Wignell (Folens Reading Pack Level 3)

Once upon a time, there was a rich man who had a fine house and garden. Behind his house and garden, he had a field of corn. One day, he noticed that some of his corn was missing.

"A robber must have come during the night to steal my corn," he said to himself. "I'll have to catch him."

The rich man called out to his three sons, Michael, George and John.

"Come here boys!" he said. "A robber is stealing my corn at night. Keep watch and I'll reward the one who catches him."

"I'll keep watch tonight," said Michael.

Michael brought some food and drink for a midnight snack. Then he lay down under a tree in his warm coat and soon fell asleep.

In the morning, he awoke with a start. He looked around nervously and saw that more corn was gone.

"Oh no!" he said.

"I'll keep watch tonight," his brother George said on the second night.

George brought a thick stick, a piece of rope and a blanket to the cornfield. He lay down under the blanket and soon fell asleep. In the morning, he also awoke with a start and looked around.

"Oh no," he said, "the robber stole more corn!"

"I'll keep watch tonight," said John, the third brother, on the third night.

John brought a rope and put a ring of thorns around his head. Every time he nodded off to sleep, the thorns pricked his nose and woke him.

At midnight, John heard a clippety-clop, clippety-clop, clippety-clop sound in the distance.

"The sound is coming closer and closer," he said to himself. "Now it's stopped in the cornfield."

John threw the ring of thorns away and crept forward, holding the rope. At last, he saw the robber!

"It's a beautiful, silvery horse!" he whispered to himself in surprise.

The horse stood still and allowed John to put a rope around its neck and take it to the stable. Then John went into the house and slept.

In the morning, Michael and George woke John up.

"You are useless!" they said. "You didn't even stay out in the field!"

John sprang up.

"Come with me," he said.

John took his father and his brothers to the stable and showed them the beautiful, silvery horse. No one knew where it had come from.

"John, you may keep the horse as a reward," said his father.

"I'm going to name him Corn Robber," John told his brothers.

UNIT 14 Activities

A Fact Finding

1. What was growing in the field behind the rich man's house?
2. How many sons did the rich man have?
3. Who was first to keep watch?
4. What did George bring with him to the cornfield?
5. What name did John give to the horse?

B Choose the word closest in meaning to the underlined word.

1. "I'll keep **watch** tonight," said Michael.
   (a) walking (b) guard
   (c) awake (d) alert
2. In the morning he awoke with a **start**.
   (a) jump (b) yawn
   (c) stretch (d) sneeze
3. The thorns **pricked** John's nose.
   (a) jabbed (b) hurt
   (c) tickled (d) rubbed
4. At midnight, John heard a sound **in the distance**.
   (a) nearby (b) next door
   (c) far away (d) outside
5. He **crept** forward.
   (a) limped (b) tiptoed
   (c) ran (d) walked
6. John's brothers told him he was **useless**.
   (a) great (b) lazy
   (c) hopeless (d) wonderful

C Choose the most suitable word to complete each sentence.

1. Once upon a time there was a rich man who had a ________ house. **(pretty, dainty, splendid, tiny)**
2. The boy's father was ________ . **(poor, wealthy, mean, heartless)**
3. "I'll ________ the son who catches the robber," said the father. **(hug, kiss, repay, prefer)**
4. Michael was ________ when he looked around. **(calm, happy, worried, weary)**
5. "It's a beautiful, silvery horse," he ________ to himself. **(murmured, moaned, grumbled, complained)**
6. John showed the ________ , silvery horse to his family. **(nice, clever, smart, magnificent)**

D

Choose the correct answer.

1. **Where was the man's field of corn?**
   (a) Behind the door.
   (b) Beside the door.
   (c) Behind the garden.
   (d) Beside the garden.
2. **Michael brought some food and drink with him because**
   (a) he might need a snack.
   (b) he wanted to feed the robber.
   (c) he wanted to feed the night animals.
   (d) his brothers might visit during the night.
3. **Why did George bring a piece of rope with him to the cornfield?**
   (a) To make a hammock with the blanket and stick.
   (b) To tie up the robber.
   (c) To skip while he waited.
   (d) To use as a marker, in case he got lost.
4. **The ring of thorns**
   (a) helped John sleep.
   (b) kept John awake.
   (c) hurt John's head.
   (d) helped catch the robber.
5. **How did John feel when he saw that the robber was a horse?**
   (a) He was angry.
   (b) He was sad.
   (c) He was surprised.
   (d) He was furious.

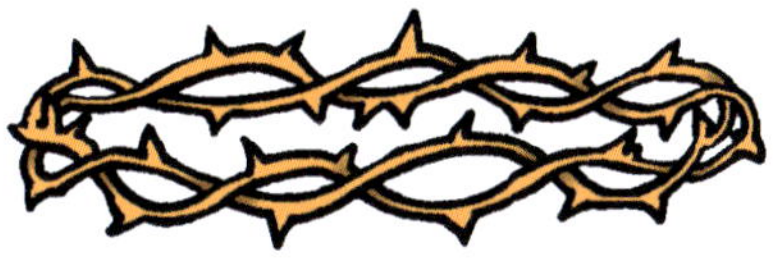

E

Grammar

Complete each sentence using nouns.

1. The rich __________ called his three __________ together.
2. "A __________ is stealing __________ from the __________," he said.
3. __________ offered to keep guard on the first __________ .
4. George brought a thick __________ and a piece of __________ with him.
5. In the middle of the __________, __________ heard a clippety-clop __________ .
6. The __________ stood still, while John put a __________ around its __________ .

F

Summarise

"I'll keep watch tonight," said John.

Read the description of John's watch and write it in your own words.

G

Use Your Imagination

Pretend you are the beautiful silver horse. You have magical powers that no one knows about yet. Write a story about how you use those powers to completely change John's life.

UNIT 15

The Little Fir Tree

A little fir tree lived in the middle of an enormous forest. There were much taller trees around her but they did not block out her light. She could feel the heat of the sun and, because she was so small, she was protected from the strong winds. Now and again little birds would land on her, but they would never stay for long. However, the little fir tree was not happy. She wanted to grow more quickly.

"If I were bigger," she thought, "I could stretch out my branches and open my leaves widely. I could see the world and the little birds would build their nests in me and stay longer."

At Christmas time, many trees were chopped down. They were placed in trailers and carried out of the forest. The little fir tree wondered where they went. One day she heard the sparrows chirping in the tall trees. She called them and asked them if they knew what happened to the trees.

"Yes," they said. "We have peeped in the windows of the houses in town and seen the trees decorated with tinsel and bright lights."

As the seasons passed the little fir tree grew big and strong, but she was still not happy. She wanted to be brought to a warm house and decorated with sparkling jewels and twinkling lights. Then, one Christmas the woodcutters arrived and chose the little fir tree. She was brought to a big house in the centre of the town, where she was decorated beautifully. The fir tree felt proud. How wonderful she felt when all the brightly wrapped presents were placed beneath her and the children danced around her in the warm glow of the fire. She knew she looked amazing, but she could not be happy. She was always wondering what might happen next.

When the excitement of Christmas came to an end, the decorations were removed from the tree and she was placed in a storeroom. The fir tree did not like the room very much. It was dark and cold. She only had the little mice who lived there for company and they wanted to know all about her life.

"What a happy time you must have had in the forest!" one said.

"Maybe," replied the tree, "but I didn't feel happy."

"And how happy you must have felt when the children decorated you and danced around you," said another mouse.

"I suppose I was," said the fir tree, "but I never felt truly happy."

After some time, the tree was brought out to the yard. The children jumped on her and broke her dried-out branches.

"How happy I was in the storeroom, where nobody bothered me," thought the tree.

Soon the tree was chopped up for firewood to be burned in the stove.

"It was nice in the yard where I had plenty of fresh air," she thought, as the fire crackled around her.

Poor little fir tree, she had lived a wonderful life but had never enjoyed it. She had never felt happiness because she had spent all her time wondering what would happen next or wishing she could return to where she had been in the past.

UNIT 15

Activities

A Fact Finding

1. Where did the little fir tree live?
2. What did she think she could do if she was bigger?
3. How did the sparrows know what happened to the trees at Christmas?
4. Who cut down the trees in the forest?
5. Why did the fir tree not like the storeroom?

B Choose the word closest in meaning to the underlined word.

1. A little fir tree lived in the middle of an **enormous** forest.
   (a) small (b) vast
   (c) tiny (d) tall
2. She was **protected** from the strong winds.
   (a) shaken (b) away
   (c) sheltered (d) hidden
3. "If I were bigger," she thought, "I could **stretch** out my branches."
   (a) push (b) blow
   (c) lift (d) spread
4. The little fir tree wanted to be decorated with **sparkling** jewels.
   (a) twinkling (b) dark
   (c) colourful (d) dull
5. The **excitement** of Christmas came to an end.
   (a) sadness (b) boredom
   (c) fun (d) season
6. How happy I was when nobody **bothered** me.
   (a) annoyed (b) heard
   (c) saw (d) pleased

C Choose the most suitable word to complete each sentence.

1. The sparrows ________ in the windows. **(peeked, fell, flew, piled)**
2. The fir tree felt ________ when she was decorated. **(happy, annoyed, honoured, afraid)**
3. The children danced around her in the warm ________ of the fire. **(smoke, crackle, redness, light)**
4. "I ________ I was," said the fir tree, "but I never felt truly happy." **(wish, know, hope, think)**

5. The children jumped on her and broke her ________ branches. **(fresh, little, broad, withered)**
6. Poor little fir tree, she had never felt ________ . **(misery, joy, fear, awe)**

D

Choose the correct answer.

1. Why was the little fir tree not happy in the forest?
   (a) She was not protected from the wind.
   (b) She had very little light.
   (c) She could not stretch her branches.
   (d) She had no friends there.

2. What happened to the trees when they left the forest?
   (a) They were chopped up.
   (b) They were decorated for Christmas.
   (c) They were used as poles.
   (d) They were used as lamps.

3. Why did the little fir tree not like the storeroom?
   (a) It was dark and cold.
   (b) She had no one to talk to.
   (c) She missed the twinkling lights.
   (d) She missed the heat of the fire.

4. What happened to the fir tree when she was in the store room?
   (a) Her branches grew leaves.
   (b) Her branches snapped.
   (c) Her branches dried out.
   (d) Her branches cracked.

5. When the fir tree was burning in the stove, she thought about
   (a) the bright decorations.
   (b) the children.
   (c) the mice.
   (d) the fresh air.

E

Grammar

Adjectives are describing words, e.g. the little tree.

Write these sentences and underline the adjectives.

1. A little tree lived in the middle of an enormous forest.
2. The large trees protected her from the strong winds.
3. The pretty birds could build their nests in her strong branches.
4. She was decorated with sparkling jewels and twinkling lights.
5. The noisy children jumped on her dried-out branches.
6. Poor little fir tree, she had lived a wonderful life but had never enjoyed it.

F

Summarise

In your own words, describe what happened to the little fir tree from when she was chosen in the forest to the end.

G

Use Your Imagination

It is Christmas. You peep in the window of a big house in the centre of the town. Write about what you see.

UNIT 16 How Fionn Became Leader of the Fianna

Long ago the High King of Ireland lived in Tara. He had a special army to protect him. They were called the Fianna. Cumhall, the Fianna's leader, had been killed by his enemy Goll MacMorna. Goll wanted to become the new leader of the Fianna.

Every Samhain (November) the king held a banquet in Tara to celebrate the harvest. Fionn, Cumhall's son, decided that he would travel to Tara in his father's place. When he arrived, he was met by the king and received a great welcome. There was silence as everybody looked at Goll, who was sitting at the long table. The king ordered his servants to set a place for Fionn. Fionn sat down beside the king's son and the feast began.

Halfway through the meal, the king spoke. "For the last nine years an evil spirit has visited Tara on this very night. It comes in the shape of a dragon. Nobody has ever been able to defeat it. Is there anybody here who will save Tara from this dangerous creature?" the king asked.

Fionn jumped to his feet.

"What reward do you offer?" he asked.

"I will give you your heart's desire," replied the king.

"In that case," said Fionn, "I will defend Tara from the evil dragon."

Everyone was amazed!

Fionn left the table and walked outside the walls of the town. It was dark and the night was still. Suddenly Fionn heard footsteps.

"Who goes there?" he shouted.

By the light of the moon, Fionn could see an old warrior standing by the wall.

"I was a friend of your father's," the warrior said. "I have come to help you. As the dragon comes close to Tara, he plays magical music. It casts a spell on all who hear the music and they fall into a deep sleep. That is why no one has been able to defeat the dragon."

"What shall I do?" asked Fionn. "How can you help me?"

The stranger handed Fionn a spear.

"Press this to your forehead as soon as the music begins," he said. "You will be protected from the dragon's magic and the music will have no power over you. You will remain awake while everyone else sleeps. The dragon will not expect that."

Then the old warrior vanished into the darkness. Fionn did not get the chance to thank him.

Many hours passed before Fionn heard the sweet sound of music. Instantly, he pressed the spear to his forehead. Just as the warrior had said, everyone in Tara fell into a deep slumber, but Fionn remained awake. The dragon landed beside Fionn. He let out a terrible roar and breathed a large flame of white hot fire! Fionn placed his feet firmly on the ground and faced the dragon, without fear. He raised the spear and aimed it at the dragon's head. He threw it. Suddenly, the dragon disappeared, never to return.

It was sunrise before the people of Tara awoke.

"What happened?" asked the king.

Fionn explained what had taken place and how the evil dragon was gone forever.

"We are grateful to you," the high king said. "You shall have your heart's desire. Please tell me what it is."

"To be leader of the Fianna, just as my father was," replied Fionn.

Goll stepped forward and put out his hand to Fionn. Fionn took it.

"I will gladly be a soldier in your army and will serve you well," Goll said.

That is how Fionn earned the right to become leader of the Fianna.

UNIT 16 Activities

A Fact Finding

1. Who lived in Tara?
2. Why was a banquet held in Tara each Samhain?
3. What shape does the evil spirit take when it visits Tara?
4. Who came to help Fionn?
5. What did Fionn aim at the dragon's head?

B Choose the word closest in meaning to the underlined word.

1. The High King had a **special** army.
   (a) normal (b) remarkable
   (c) cowardly (d) strange
2. Every Samhain the king held a **banquet** in Tara.
   (a) birthday party (b) wedding
   (c) dance (d) feast
3. Who will save Tara from this dangerous **creature**?
   (a) monster (b) bear
   (c) person (d) magic
4. It was dark and the night was **still**.
   (a) cold (b) quiet
   (c) noisy (d) stormy
5. Fionn saw an old **warrior** standing by a wall.
   (a) man (b) person
   (c) soldier (d) creature
6. **Instantly**, he pressed the spear to his forehead.
   (a) immediately (b) slowly
   (c) quickly (d) swiftly

C Choose the most suitable word to complete each sentence.

1. Nobody has ever been able to ________ the dragon. **(conquer, love, meet, understand)**
2. Everyone was ________ when Fionn said he would defend Tara. **(happy, thrilled, astonished, annoyed)**
3. The old warrior ________ into the darkness. **(walked, faded, melted, disappeared)**
4. Everyone in Tara fell into a deep ________. **(well, sleep, hole, lake)**
5. He raised the spear and ________ it at the dragon. **(threw, pointed, lobbed, cast)**
6. "You shall have your heart's ________," the king said. **(wish, thoughts, needs, feelings)**

D

Choose the correct answer.

1. **Why did the king hold a banquet?**
   (a) To celebrate Hallowe'en.
   (b) To celebrate the harvest.
   (c) To celebrate Easter.
   (d) To celebrate his birthday.

2. **The king gave Fionn a great welcome because**
   (a) he had not been to Tara before.
   (b) he had not seen him since his father had been killed.
   (c) he had not seen him since his father had won the battle.
   (d) he had not seen him since he had fought the dragon.

3. **Why could no one defeat the dragon?**
   (a) It sent everyone to sleep.
   (b) It was too strong.
   (c) The Fianna were afraid.
   (d) The Fianna were at a party.

4. **What protected Fionn from the dragon's magic?**
   (a) The warrior's voice.
   (b) The moon.
   (c) The king's army.
   (d) The spear.

5. **When Fionn saw the dragon, he was**
   (a) afraid. (b) not afraid.
   (c) scared. (d) surprised.

E

Grammar

Complete each sentence using a suitable adjective.

1. The high king of Ireland had a ________ army to protect him.
2. Fionn received a ________ welcome before sitting at the ________ table.
3. "I will defend Tara from the ________ dragon," said ________ Fionn.
4. The ________ music will have no ________ power over you.
5. The ________ warrior vanished into the ________ night.

F

Character Description

It must have taken great courage for Fionn to sit beside Goll.

Read the story again. Write a short paragraph describing the type of person you think Fionn was.

G

Explore the Text

This story is a legend. Legends are often stories about people who overcome evil.

Name the main characters in the story. What evil had to be overcome? How was this done?

UNIT 17 Surviving in the Tundra

From *Surviving in the Tundra* by Tracey Michele (Folens Reading Pack Level 3)

Introduction

The tundra is the name given to flat plains in the Arctic. It is very cold in the tundra and the winds are icy. The winter is long and cold, and the summer is short and cool. The ground is frozen all year round, so not many plants can grow.

Purple = Tundra

Tundra

In the short summer, a thin layer of ice melts and forms pools and streams. Some plants such as shrubs, moss and grass grow.

Only a few centimetres of tundra ice melts in summer.

Only plants with short roots can grow in the tundra summer.

Tundra Animals

Animals in the tundra have different ways of coping with the cold. Many tundra animals have thick fur. Some tundra animals have extra layers of fat to keep them warm in winter. Some tundra animals have hair on the bottom of their feet. The hair helps them move around safely on the ice.

Some tundra animals make tunnels in the snow called burrows. Burrows help them hide from the cold wind. Other tundra animals move into large holes, called dens, when there are strong snowstorms.

Musk Oxen

Musk oxen are animals that are found in the tundra in Greenland and Canada. They have an outer coat and an inner coat that keep them warm. The outer coat has dark brown hair and hangs down to their feet. The inner coat is next to their skin. It is pale brown and woolly. In spring, musk oxen lose the woolly undercoat. It grows again in autumn to keep them warm in winter.

Polar Bears

Polar bears are found in the tundra in Canada, Alaska, Greenland and Russia.

Polar bears have thick fur. Under the fur is a layer of fat that keeps them warm. Some of the outer fur has hollow hairs. When the sun shines, the heat can get through the hollow hairs to warm the polar bears' skin.

Polar bears have short, stiff hairs on the bottom of their feet. These hairs stop them from slipping on the ice.

Female polar bears make dens where they stay in winter to give birth to cubs.

Polar bears hunt seals for food. A polar bear waits on the edge of the ice for a seal to come up for air and grabs it quickly.

Arctic Hares

Arctic hares are found in the tundra in Canada and Greenland. They are small animals that grow up to 50 cm long.

In summer, Arctic hares have a grey-brown coat. But in winter, it changes to white except for black on the tips of the ears. The white coat helps Arctic hares hide from predators (enemies).

In summer, Arctic hares eat grass, leaves and twigs. In winter, they eat woody stems and bark. They use their strong claws to dig through the snow. Arctic hares also have large feet that keep them from sinking in the snow.

An Arctic hare's winter coat keeps it warm and safe in the icy weather.

UNIT 17

Activities

A

Fact Finding

1. What is the name given to flat plains in the Arctic?
2. What type of plants grow in the tundra summer?
3. Where would you find musk oxen?
4. Why do polar bears not slip on ice?
5. When does the Arctic hare's coat change colour?

B

Choose the word closest in meaning to the underlined word.

1. The map shows the **location** of the tundra.
   (a) picture (b) colour
   (c) position (d) size
2. In the short summer, a thin **layer** of ice melts.
   (a) sheet (b) lump
   (c) block (d) cube
3. Animals in the tundra have ways of **coping** with the cold.
   (a) playing (b) arguing
   (c) being (d) dealing
4. A polar bear waits for a seal to come up for air and **grabs** it.
   (a) steals (b) touches
   (c) snatches (d) smells
5. The white coat helps Arctic hares hide from **predators**.
   (a) friends (b) enemies
   (c) mates (d) pals
6. This unit starts with an **introduction**.
   (a) ending (b) picture
   (c) conversation (d) opening

C

Choose the most suitable word to complete each sentence.

1. Some ice melts and ________ pools. **(draws, makes, grows, freezes)**
2. The musk oxen's second coat is ________ their skin. **(over, under, hurting, beside)**
3. When the sun shines, the heat can get through the ________ hairs to warm the polar bear's skin. **(thick, thin, curly, unfilled)**
4. This unit is about how animals ________ in the tundra. **(dance, eat, survive, sleep)**
5. Female polar bears make ________ in the snow. **(houses, holes, setts, nests)**
6. Arctic hares have large feet that keep them from ________ in the snow. **(disappearing, appearing, skiing, falling)**

D Choose the correct answer.

1. In the tundra, the winter

(a) is long and wet.
(b) is short and cool.
(c) is long and cold.
(d) is short and wet.

2. How do some animals cope with the cold?

(a) They wear warm coats.
(b) They have extra layers of fat.
(c) They have extra layers of fur.
(d) They grow extra layers of skin.

3. Some animals hide from the wind

(a) in nests.
(b) in sheds.
(c) in out-houses.
(d) in tunnels.

4. Which of these countries does not have polar bears?

(a) Canada.
(b) South Africa.
(c) Greenland.
(d) Russia.

5. In winter the Arctic hare's coat changes to white with black on

(a) the tips of the ears.
(b) the tip of the nose.
(c) the tips of the claws.
(d) the tips of the eyelids.

E Grammar

To, two and too. I am going <u>to</u> make a tunnel. The bear gave birth to <u>two</u> cubs. The fox did <u>too</u>.

Choose the correct word to finish the sentences.

1. The tundra is the name given _________ plains in the Arctic. **(two, to)**
2. Musk oxen have _________ coats. **(too, two)**
3. The heat gets through _________ the polar bear's warm skin. **(to, too)**
4. Musk oxen are found in Greenland and Canada. Arctic hares are found there _________ . **(to, two, too)**
5. Female polar bears give birth _________ their cubs in dens. **(to, too)**
6. The Arctic hare's winter coat keeps it warm in icy weather and keeps it safe from predators _________ . **(to, two, too)**

F Summarise

Read the paragraph which describes the different ways tundra animals have of coping with the cold. Pick out the important points and rewrite it in three sentences.

G Use Your Imagination

Imagine you are a polar bear living in Dublin Zoo. You grew up in the tundra. Tell your friends what it was like living in the tundra.

UNIT 18 Clumsy Clinton

From *Clumsy Clinton* by Alan Horsfield (Folens Reading Pack Level 3)

He turned up with a big, sunny smile on his face. Mum peeped through the curtains.

"It's Uncle Clinton! With a suitcase!" she whispered, wide-eyed. "On our doorstep!"

"We're in for a few laughs then!" said Dad with a smile.

"Why's that?" I asked.

"My brother's always been so clumsy he's dangerous," replied Dad.

"He's just a bit awkward," said Mum. Then she smiled at me. "Answer the door, Misty."

"Just be careful, Misty!" said Dad, smiling. "Clinton can be quite clumsy."

I went to the front door to greet Uncle Clinton. His hair had grown a lot since I last saw him. He wore bright yellow trousers with wide braces. I couldn't imagine Dad would ever wear trousers like that, even when his leg was better. Uncle Clinton's bright, flowery shirt dazzled me. His black cap hardly seemed to fit on his head and his brown shoes seemed far too big for his feet. Something about his clothes and hair reminded me of something or someone, but I couldn't think what it was.

There was a twinkle in Uncle Clinton's eye even though he tripped coming through the door into our living room to say hello to Mum and Dad.

It was at lunch that I saw how Uncle Clinton was more than clumsy. He seemed to be absent-minded, too. Instead of looking at what he was doing, he looked away and whistled. The juice he was pouring didn't even go into the glass. I kept wondering if he was doing it on purpose and why Mum and Dad weren't mad at him.

"Misty, why don't you and Uncle Clinton take Scruffy for a walk?" Dad said as soon as lunch was over.

Uncle Clinton smiled his sunny smile.

As we left the house, I heard Dad say again, "He's always been so clumsy he's dangerous!"

"Maybe just a bit awkward," said Mum.

Uncle Clinton heard what they said, and just when I thought his sunny smile would turn into a grey cloud, he winked at me and said, "Being clumsy can be useful!"

I didn't know what to do or say, so I gave Uncle Clinton Scruffy's leash.

Before we knew it, Scruffy had wrapped her leash around Uncle Clinton's big, brown shoes. He tried to step away, but before I could steady him, he tumbled and sat down on the path and his cap blew away. I untangled Scruffy and unclipped her leash and she bounded after the cap. Once again, I was reminded of something, but I didn't know what. Maybe it was the way Uncle Clinton smiled as he fell.

I looked at Uncle Clinton and he looked at me, and then we sat on the grass. Soon, Scruffy came back with Uncle Clinton's battered cap in her mouth. Uncle Clinton put it on before I could stop him. Yuk! The way he put his cap on again reminded me of something or someone.

Later, I told Dad and Mum what had happened and again Dad said, "He's always been so clumsy he's dangerous."

"Well, maybe just a bit awkward," Mum said.

UNIT 18 Activities

A Fact Finding

1. Who turned up with a sunny smile on his face?
2. Who greeted Clinton at the door?
3. What colour trousers did Clinton wear?
4. At what meal did Misty see how clumsy Clinton was?
5. Why did Clinton end up on the path with no hat?

B Choose the word closest in meaning to the underlined word.

1. Mum peeped through the **curtains**.
   (a) drapes (b) door
   (c) sill (d) windows
2. Clinton is just a bit **awkward**.
   (a) careful (b) clumsy
   (c) funny (d) tricky
3. Misty went to **greet** Uncle Clinton.
   (a) see (b) welcome
   (c) wave at (d) befriend
4. Uncle Clinton's bright, flowery shirt **dazzled** me.
   (a) deafened (b) impressed
   (c) blinded (d) cheered
5. He seemed to be **absent-minded**.
   (a) alert (b) clever
   (c) smart (d) forgetful
6. Misty gave Clinton Scruffy's **leash**.
   (a) collar (b) lead
   (c) bone (d) coat

C Choose the most suitable word to complete each sentence.

1. I couldn't ________ Dad wearing trousers like Clinton's.
   (understand, allow, picture, paint)
2. I kept wondering if Clinton was spilling the juice ________.
   (accidentally, purposely, carefully, absent-mindedly)
3. "He's always been so clumsy, he's ________," said Dad.
   (safe, harmless, awkward, unsafe)
4. Scruffy ________ her leash around Clinton's shoes.
   (twisted, placed, put, threw)
5. Before I could steady him, he ________ and sat on the path.
   (laughed, smiled, fell, shouted)
6. Soon Scruffy came back with Uncle Clinton's ________ cap.
   (new, scruffy, clean, dazzling)

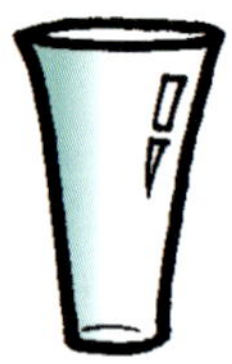

D Choose the correct answer.

1. Why did Dad smile when he saw Clinton?

(a) He knew Clinton would make him sad.

(b) He knew Clinton would make him crazy.

(c) He knew Clinton would make him laugh.

(d) He knew Clinton would make him cry.

2. What happened as Clinton came into the living room?

(a) He fell.

(b) He jumped.

(c) He smiled.

(d) He laughed.

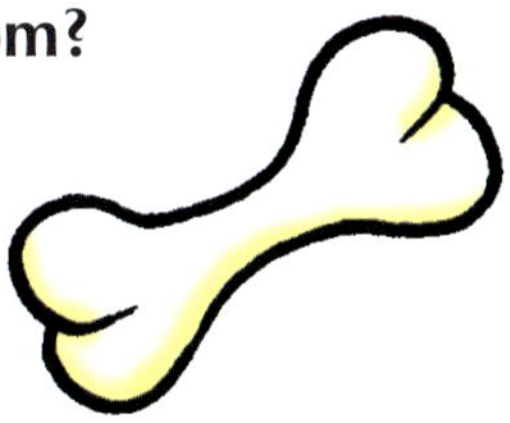

3. Which sentence is true?

(a) Clinton drank the juice.

(b) Clinton enjoyed the juice.

(c) Clinton hated the juice.

(d) Clinton spilt the juice.

4. Misty and Clinton took Scruffy

(a) for a bone.

(b) for a walk.

(c) for a jog.

(d) for an ice cream.

5. When Scruffy was unclipped, she

(a) ate the cap.

(b) ripped the cap.

(c) ran after the cap.

(d) buried the cap.

E Grammar

"Its" means "belonging to it", e.g. Its bright colours dazzled me.
"It's" means "it is", e.g. It's Clinton with a suitcase!

Write "Its" or "It's" to complete these sentences.

1. _________ dangerous when Clinton is around.
2. The yellow trousers were held up by _________ wide braces.
3. " _________ time to bring Scruffy for a walk," said Dad.
4. Before _________ leash was removed, the dog ran after the cap.
5. The cap was battered and _________ peak was torn.
6. "Sometimes _________ useful being clumsy," Clinton said.

F Character Description

We know from the name of the story that Clinton was clumsy.
Read the story again and make a list of all the examples of Clinton's clumsiness.

G Use Your Imagination

Misty wondered if Clinton was being clumsy on purpose. What do you think?

UNIT 19

Tamlin's Rescue

As dawn broke over the dark hills, a beautiful sound filled the air. Tamlin, the most wonderful musician of all, was playing lovely, calm music on his flute. The birds and animals of the forest became still. Slowly they came closer to listen.

As Tamlin continued to play his flute, a beautiful lady appeared. She had been walking in the forest and was drawn to the magical music. Her name was Janet and Tamlin instantly fell in love with her. He wanted to marry her but his heart was heavy, for he knew they could not wed.

Many years earlier the Queen of the Fairies had cast a spell on him. She had changed him into an elf and he belonged to her. He could not give his heart to another woman. Janet loved Tamlin too and she promised to do all she could to rescue him from the Fairy Queen.

At Hallowe'en, fairies become visible in our world. They mount their magical horses and ride across the land. Tamlin knew that he could only be rescued on that night.

"At midnight on Hallowe'en, I will ride through the forest with the Queen at my side," Tamlin told Janet. "She and the other fairies will be riding white horses. Mine will be the only black horse. You must grab me and hold on tight. I will change shape many times. No matter what happens do not let go," he warned her.

Janet returned home to wait. She was afraid, but she decided to do what her true love had asked.

While she waited for Hallowe'en, Janet made a beautiful wedding dress. On Hallowe'en night, she put it on and walked to the forest. She hid behind some bushes.

After some time she saw a golden mist creeping through the trees. She knew at once that the fairies had arrived. As the mist cleared Janet saw the Fairy Queen. She was dressed in a beautiful gown, with pearls in her hair. Janet's true love, Tamlin, was riding beside her.

Janet jumped out from behind the bushes where she had been waiting. Her heart was thumping. She dragged Tamlin off his fairy horse. The Fairy Queen screamed. Her face became ugly.

"He is mine," the Fairy Queen screeched. "You shall not have him!"

She pointed her magic wand at Tamlin and he immediately changed into a spitting, wriggling, slimy snake. Janet was afraid, but she remembered Tamlin's words and held on tightly. The Queen raised her wand again and the snake became an ugly, biting rat. Although Janet was scared, she would not give up. The Queen continued to wave her wand. Tamlin changed into a powerful eagle which clawed at Janet and flapped its enormous wings. Then Tamlin changed into a tiger cub, which scratched and scraped Janet. Next the cub changed into a slippery salmon.

Janet clutched each creature firmly. The Fairy Queen became more and more enraged. She pointed her wand for one last time. A fierce, wild bear appeared. Janet struggled to hold on to the bear, but she never gave up. Finally the creature disappeared. It was replaced by Tamlin. The Fairy Queen could not believe it. She galloped away, shouting loudly. Her army of fairies rode quickly behind her.

Janet fell to the ground. She was so tired. Tamlin bent down, gently picked her up and kissed her.

"You saved me," he said.

Before her very eyes he became a handsome knight.

"We shall be married at midnight," he said.

And so they were.

UNIT 19 Activities

A Fact Finding

1. What instrument did Tamlin play?
2. Why was Tamlin's heart heavy?
3. What colour horse would the Fairy Queen be riding?
4. What was Janet wearing while in the forest?
5. Name the creatures into which Tamlin changed.

B Choose the word closest in meaning to the underlined word.

1. Tamlin was playing **calm** music.
   (a) loud (b) peaceful
   (c) magical (d) pretty
2. Tamlin **instantly** fell in love with Janet.
   (a) suddenly (b) often
   (c) immediately (d) quickly
3. Janet was **afraid**.
   (a) scared (b) horrified
   (c) unsure (d) calm
4. She knew at once the fairies had **arrived**.
   (a) peeked (b) run
   (c) chuckled (d) come
5. Janet **clutched** each creature firmly.
   (a) grasped (b) carried
   (c) snatched (d) spoke to
6. The Queen became more **enraged**.
   (a) ugly (b) angry
   (c) scary (d) afraid

C Choose the most suitable word to complete each sentence.

1. Janet was ________ to the magical music. **(dancing, attracted, singing, humming)**
2. Many years ________ Tamlin had come under the Fairy Queen's spell. **(since, ago, earlier, later)**
3. "Mine will be the only black ________," Tamlin said. **(horse, creature, animal, mare)**
4. The Queen wore a ________ gown. **(lovely, splendid, nice, pretty)**
5. "He is mine," the Fairy Queen ________. **(said, laughed, screamed, whispered)**
6. A fierce, ________ bear appeared. **(wild, weary, wise, tame)**

D

Choose the correct answer.

1. Tamlin could not wed Janet because

(a) he did not love her.

(b) he loved the Fairy Queen.

(c) he was under the Fairy Queen's spell.

(d) he was under the music's spell.

2. Why was Hallowe'en the only time Tamlin could be rescued?

(a) The fairies became invisible.

(b) The fairies became visible.

(c) It was the only time Janet could go to the forest

(d) It was the only time Janet was ready.

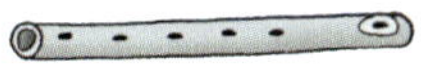

3. How did Janet become aware of the army of fairies?

(a) She saw a golden mist.

(b) She heard the horses' hooves.

(c) She heard the sound of voices.

(d) She heard the Queen's voice.

4. When the queen of the fairies screamed, "He is mine," she meant:

(a) I love him.

(b) Go away.

(c) He belongs to me.

(d) He works for me.

5. As Janet clutched each creature firmly, the Queen became more

(a) amazed. (b) angry.

(c) anxious. (d) worried.

E

Grammar

Verbs are action words, e.g. Tamlin was playing music on his flute. Write these sentences and underline the verbs.

1. Janet was walking in the forest and heard the magical music.
2. Fairies mount their magical horses and ride across the land.
3. She put on her wedding dress, walked to the forest and hid behind bushes.
4. Her heart was thumping as she dragged Tamlin off his horse.
5. The Fairy Queen galloped away, shouting loudly.
6. Tamlin bent down, gently picked Janet up and kissed her.

F

Summarise

Tamlin describes what would happen at Hallowe'en. In your own words describe what Janet would have to do to rescue Tamlin.

G

Character Description

In the story we learn that the Fairy Queen was beautiful. Read the story again. What type of person do you think the Fairy Queen was? Write a short paragraph describing her.

UNIT 20

Chinese New Year

From *Chinese New Year* by Edel Wignell (Folens Reading Pack Level 3)

People all around the world celebrate the new year in different ways. Many people celebrate New Year's Eve on December 31 and New Year's Day on January 1. But some countries, such as China, celebrate the New Year at a different time of the year. Each year, the Chinese New Year date is different because it depends on the cycle of the moon. Chinese New Year begins with the new moon and can start between January 21 and February 20. The celebrations last for 15 days.

Chinese New Year Traditions

The Chinese do special things each year at New Year. These are called traditions. Many people do housework before the new year. Doing housework clears away the dirt from last year and is a symbol of clearing away last year's bad luck. People may then decorate their clean houses with flowers. The flowers are a symbol of a fresh start.

Many Chinese visit their relatives during the 15-day New Year celebrations. People also give gifts to their family and friends to celebrate New Year. Some special gifts that they give are packets of fortune cookies, little red envelopes with "lucky money" inside, and eight oranges or eight mandarins. One wish for a Happy New Year is "Gong Xi Fa Cai." ("We wish you great wealth.")

Another Chinese tradition is the special food that people eat at New Year. Many people prepare a large feast before New Year. Families then eat this food together on New Year's Eve. The large amount of food is a symbol of lots of food and wealth for the year ahead.

Most of the food has special meanings. One special food is dumplings. The dumplings are called jiaozi in Chinese. These dumplings are often made in the shape of gold nuggets and are a symbol of good luck. It is a tradition for family members to make the dumplings together.

Another special food that the Chinese eat at New Year is a dessert called nian gao. Nian gao is a New Year cake made from rice flour and brown sugar. The Chinese eat it to bring good luck.

Some foods have names that in Chinese sound like "luck" or "wealth". So the Chinese eat these foods at New Year to bring them luck and wealth in the year head. For example, the Chinese word for fish sounds like the word that means "more than enough".

Origin of the Chinese New Year

There are several stories that explain the history of the Chinese New Year. One describes the celebrations as a spring festival. The New Year marks the end of one farming season and the beginning of a new one.

Another story describes how, long ago, a person named Buddha asked all the animals to come to a meeting. Only 12 animals came. Buddha rewarded them by naming a year after each animal in the order in which they came to the meeting. They were the rat, ox, tiger, rabbit, dragon, snake, horse, sheep, monkey, rooster, dog and pig. So that means the Chinese calendar covers 12 years.

UNIT 20

Activities

A Fact Finding

1. For how long do the Chinese New Year celebrations last?
2. Why do many people clean their houses before the new year?
3. What is nian gao?
4. How many animals came to the meeting arranged by Buddha?
5. Which was the fifth animal to arrive at the meeting?

B Choose the word closest in meaning to the underlined word.

1. People celebrate the new year in **different** ways.
   (a) similar (b) various
   (c) unusual (d) strange
2. The Chinese New Year date **depends** on the moon.
   (a) rains (b) trusts
   (c) looks (d) relies
3. Doing housework is a **symbol** of clearing away last year's bad luck.
   (a) way (b) method
   (c) sign (d) mark
4. Another Chinese **tradition** is special food for New Year.
   (a) custom (b) dish
   (c) action (d) word
5. The word for fish sounds like the word for "more than **enough**".
   (a) ever (b) yesterday
   (c) desired (d) needed
6. The last section of this unit is called **Origin** of the Chinese New Year.
   (a) end (b) traditions
   (c) beginning (d) finish

C Choose the most suitable word to complete each sentence.

1. The ________ for the Chinese New Year last for 15 days. **(partying, noise, parades, dragons)**
2. Many Chinese visit their ________ during the 15-day celebrations. **(friends, priests, family, enemies)**
3. The jiaozi are shaped like gold ________ . **(chunks, chains, cups, earrings)**
4. ________ stories tell the history of New Year. **(Some, Few, Many, No)**
5. One story ________ the New Year celebrations as a spring festival. **(ignores, explains, recalls, names)**
6. Buddha gave each animal the ________ of naming a year after each one of them. **(joy, job, challenge, gift)**

D

Choose the correct answer.

1. The Chinese New Year celebrations last a little longer than

(a) a month. (b) a fortnight.

(c) a year. (d) a decade.

2. People decorate their houses with flowers because

(a) they are a symbol of beauty.

(b) they are a symbol of cleanliness.

(c) they are a symbol of riches.

(d) they are a symbol of new beginnings.

3. Chinese people eat foods which sound like "luck" or "wealth" at New Year

(a) to bring them bad luck in the year ahead.

(b) to bring them happiness in the year ahead.

(c) to bring them good luck in the year ahead.

(d) to bring them no luck in the year ahead.

4. One of the many stories describing the Chinese New Year calls it

(a) a spring festival.

(b) a winter festival.

(c) a summer festival.

(d) an autumn festival.

5. Which animal did not attend the meeting?

(a) Pig. (b) Monkey.

(c) Lion. (d) Dragon.

E

Grammar

Write verbs for these sentences.

1. The Chinese New Year ________ with the new moon.
2. People ________ their houses with flowers.
3. People also ________ gifts to their families and friends.
4. It is a tradition for family members to ________ the dumplings together.
5. The New Year ________ the end of the farming year.
6. Buddha ________ all the animals to come to a meeting.

F

Summarise

A number of Chinese New Year traditions are described in this piece. Read them again and write a short summary of the traditions in your own words.

G

Explore the Text

There are many different types of writing. This is an information piece. It gives you factual information. Read the piece again and make a list of five things you have learned about the Chinese New Year.

UNIT 21 The Dreamer

Amy was a dreamer. She loved to dream about ways of changing her life. Her biggest wish was to be wealthy and to be able to buy lots of computer games without having to save for them. For many months now she had been thinking long and hard about how she could make this happen. One day she came up with a plan.

Amy's aunt kept hens.

"If I helped you collect the eggs in the mornings, could I keep some of them?" she asked her aunt.

"Of course, Amy," her aunt replied. "We never manage to use all the eggs those hens lay."

Within two days Amy had managed to gather a dozen eggs for herself. She thanked her aunt, placed the eggs in a basket and headed for home. On her way, she stopped to pick blackberries from the briars that grew in the ditch. She put the basket of eggs carefully in the ditch and began to eat the blackberries. As she was eating them, she started to daydream about her clever plan.

If all the eggs hatched, she would have twelve chickens. She could take care of them and when they grew up they would lay eggs for her. She could sell the eggs and if she saved very hard, she might have enough money to buy a cow. Then she would also have milk to sell.

"I could make cheese with the milk," Amy thought. "Then I could get my own stall at the farmers' market in town and sell eggs, milk and homemade cheese."

Amy reckoned if she worked hard enough and sold enough produce, she should soon be able to buy a small field and have a small house built on it.

She would sell the house, make enough money to buy more land and build more houses. Then she could sell or rent the houses. Amy could feel herself getting excited as the ideas came rushing into her head. One thought was being replaced very quickly by another!

"Horses!" she thought "I would be able to buy horses with all that money and maybe set up a riding school and have lots of people working for me."

Oh, what wonderful dreams she was having! Amy then came to a conclusion. If she had enough people working for her, she wouldn't have to work herself.

"How wonderful," she thought.

She could buy an expensive house with a games' room, tennis courts, stables and a swimming pool. She would not have to go to school any more. She could spend her days swimming, playing tennis and riding her horses. Her friends would all come to her fine house and play computer games all day long. She would never have to make her bed or do any chores ever again because her servants would do everything she told them to do. Amy's life was really starting to look wonderful. She could have all the riches she dreamed about and live the pampered life she so wanted.

Feeling tired as a result of all her thinking and dreaming, Amy decided to sit down in the ditch and rest before finishing her walk home. As she went to sit down she never looked behind her. What did she end up sitting on? The basket of eggs! Amy's dreams had brought her so far into the future that she had forgotten about the eggs which were in the present. They were all smashed.

"Oh no!" Amy cried.

Her eggs and dreams lay in pieces on the side of the road!

UNIT 21

Activities

A Fact Finding

1. What was Amy's biggest wish?
2. How long did it take Amy to collect a dozen eggs for herself?
3. What was Amy eating as she thought about her clever plan?
4. Where could Amy sell her eggs, milk and cheese?
5. How did Amy's eggs break?

B Choose the word closest in meaning to the underlined word.

1. Amy wanted to be **wealthy**.
   (a) healthy (b) poor
   (c) wise (d) rich
2. One day Amy came up with a **plan**.
   (a) drawing (b) idea
   (c) picture (d) reason
3. Amy had **gathered** a dozen eggs.
   (a) collected (b) broken
   (c) smashed (d) dropped
4. If she sold enough **produce**, she might be able to buy a small field.
   (a) sweets (b) chocolate
   (c) people (d) items
5. She wanted an **expensive** house.
   (a) enormous (b) extra
   (c) dear (d) exciting
6. Amy could live a **pampered** life.
   (a) silly (b) comfortable
   (c) crazy (d) tough

C Choose the most suitable word to complete each sentence.

1. Amy's aunt was never ________ to use all the hens' eggs. **(awake, able, allowed, there)**
2. She put the basket of eggs in the ditch and ________ to eat the blackberries. **(stopped, decided, planned, began)**
3. One thought was being ________ by another. **(swapped, swallowed, lost, forgotten)**
4. She would never have to do any ________ ever again. **(shopping, playing, jobs, homework)**
5. Amy decided to sit in the ditch before ________ her walk home. **(starting, running, ending, doing)**
6. The eggs were all ________. **(boiled, broken, chipped, cracked)**

D

Choose the correct answer.

1. **How many eggs did Amy manage to gather?**
   (a) One. (b) Twelve.
   (c) Thirteen. (d) Twenty-four.
2. **What did Amy start to do as she was eating blackberries?**
   (a) She started to feel sick.
   (b) She started to feel thirsty.
   (c) She started to feel tired.
   (d) She started to feel scared.
3. **What could Amy sell at the farmers' market?**
   (a) Bananas, apples and pears.
   (b) Potatoes, carrots and broccoli.
   (c) Eggs, milk and cheese
   (d) Pasta, rice and bread.
4. **Who would do everything Amy told them to do?**
   (a) Her servants.
   (b) Her parents.
   (c) Her friends.
   (d) Her teachers.

5. **How did Amy smash the eggs?**
   (a) She stood on them.
   (b) She dropped them.
   (c) She fell on them.
   (d) She sat on them.

E

Grammar

Comparing words: Quick – Quicker – Quickest

Write the correct word to finish the sentences.

1. Amy's __________ wish was to be wealthy. **(big, biggest)**
2. She would be __________ than her friends. **(richer, richest)**
3. You must work __________ to earn lots of money. **(hard, hard[illegible])**
4. She would be able to swim __________ than her friends. **(fastest, faster)**
5. Amy could own the __________ house in the world. **(large, larger, largest)**
6. Amy was very __________ when she smashed the eggs. **(sad, sadder, saddest)**

F

Summarise

Make a list of Amy's many ideas. Using this list, write a short paragraph describing how Amy planned to afford a pampered life.

G

Use Your Imagination

Amy loved to dream about ways of changing her life. If you could have anything you want, what would it be? How might you get it or make it happen? Write a story about your dreams.

UNIT 22

The Frightened Scarecrow

From *The Frightened Scarecrow* by Alan Horsfield (Folens Reading Pack Level 3)

When he was finished, Jake took his scarecrow to a grassy patch near the cornfield. He pushed it into the ground and then stepped back to admire his work. The scarecrow was as tall as he was and it looked scary.

"Hold your head high and scare away the birds!" Jake told the scarecrow.

But the next morning the sky over the cornfield was crowded with large, black birds again. There were birds everywhere. They were clinging to the cornstalks and ripping open the corncobs. Some were even sitting on the scarecrow.

Then Jake saw that his scarecrow had hung its head.

"What's up, scarecrow?" he asked.

"I'm scared," the scarecrow replied without looking up.

Gently, Jake pushed the scarecrow's head up.

"You're not supposed to be scared. You're supposed to be scaring the birds," he said. "You can't scare birds if you hang your head like that."

"But last night was very dark," whispered the scarecrow.

"There's nothing to be scared of in the dark," said Jake.

"But I could hear strange noises," the scarecrow said with tears in its eyes.

"It was probably rabbits, or owls in the trees," explained Jake. "Now, just hold your head up high and scare the birds."

Later, Jake told his dad about the scarecrow. Jake's dad shook his head and frowned.

"We need to get that scarecrow to scare the birds," he said, "or we'll have no corn crop at all."

It was raining the next morning, so Jake put on his raincoat and went to check on the corn. The scarecrow's head was down again and there were birds everywhere.

"Why aren't you scaring away the birds?" Jake called.

"My clothes are wet, I'm cold, spiders are making webs under my arms, there are mice in my pockets and I'm still scared," the scarecrow replied sadly.

"So what are you scared of now?" Jake asked.

"The birds," answered the scarecrow. "The big, black birds keep looking at me and some little, brown birds are making a nest in my hat."

"You really do need some help, don't you?" said Jake kindly.

He found an old plastic sheet, which he put around the scarecrow's neck like a cape.

"That'll keep you dry," he said.

Then, he shooed away the little, brown birds and the spiders and took the mice out of the scarecrow's pockets.

"That's better," said Jake, stepping back. "You'll be okay now. All you have to do is hold your head up high and scare the black birds off the corn."

"Couldn't I come and stay in the farmhouse with you?" asked the scarecrow, still looking sad.

"You can't come and live in the farmhouse," replied Jake. "I made you to scare the birds off the corn and that's what you have to do. But I have an idea. I always feel braver when I'm with my friend. Now, hold your head up and I'll be back later in the day."

UNIT 22

Activities

A Fact Finding

1. Where did Jake put the scarecrow?
2. What did Jake tell the scarecrow to do?
3. Who did Jake talk to about the scarecrow?
4. What did Jake use to keep the scarecrow dry?
5. What helps Jake feel brave?

B Choose the word closest in meaning to the underlined word.

1. Jake stepped back to **admire** his work.
   (a) despise (b) see
   (c) marvel at (d) forget
2. "Hold your head high and **scare** away the birds," said Jake.
   (a) frighten (b) push
   (c) shoo (d) blow
3. You're not **supposed** to be scared.
   (a) allowed (b) able
   (c) asked (d) meant
4. Jake's dad shook his head and **frowned**.
   (a) smiled (b) scowled
   (c) laughed (d) growled
5. "The birds are scaring me," **answered** the scarecrow.
   (a) whispered (b) said
   (c) replied (d) announced
6. I always feel **brave** when I'm with my friend.
   (a) fearless (b) fearful
   (c) afraid (d) happier

C Choose the most suitable word to complete each sentence.

1. The scarecrow was as __________ as Jake. **(small, thin, big, short)**
2. The sky over the cornfield was __________ with large, black birds. **(filled, bright, dazzled, wet)**
3. The birds were __________ the corn stalks. **(eating, watching, grasping, breaking)**
4. The scarecrow was scared because he could hear __________ noises. **(funny, weird, loud, soft)**
5. Jake's dad was __________ about his crop of corn. **(joking, happy, sad, worried)**
6. The scarecrow wanted to stay in the __________ . **(barn, house, shed, field)**

D

Choose the correct answer.

1. **The birds were clinging to the corn stalks and**
   (a) eating the corn cobs.
   (b) nibbling the corn cobs.
   (c) tearing open the corn cobs.
   (d) looking at the corn cobs.
2. **Of what was the scarecrow afraid?**
   (a) The corn. (b) The rabbits.
   (c) The farmhouse. (d) The dark.
3. **Jake's dad frowned because**
   (a) he was angry.
   (b) he was cross.
   (c) he was concerned.
   (d) he was annoyed.
4. **How did the scarecrow's clothes get wet?**
   (a) Jake had sprayed him with water.
   (b) It had rained.
   (c) He had been swimming in his clothes.
   (d) He had fallen in the wet field.
5. **Jake told the scarecrow, he would**
   (a) return later.
   (b) not return at all.
   (c) return when it was dark.
   (d) return in the morning.

E

Grammar

No is the opposite of yes, e.g. "No!" said the scarecrow. Know is to have knowledge, e.g. "I know you are afraid," said Jake.

Choose the correct word to complete the sentences.

1. "I ________ you can do this work," Jake told the scarecrow.
2. "________, I can't," said the scarecrow.
3. "There is ________ way we can let the birds eat the corn," Jake said.
4. "I don't ________ what to do!" cried Jake.
5. "I ________ what I'm afraid of," the scarecrow told Jake.
6. "I feel ________ fear when I'm with friends," said Jake.

F

Character Description

"Gently, Jake pushed the scarecrow's head up." This tells us that Jake was a gentle boy.
Find other sentences in the story which tell us more about Jake. Write them out and explain what you learned about Jake's character.

G

Use Your Imagination

It is a wet night. The doorbell rings. You answer it and standing there is Scarecrow. "Please let me in," he says. "I'm wet and very scared."
Continue the story.

UNIT 23 Animals Growing and Changing

From *Growing and Changing* by Pamela Graham (Folens Reading Pack Level 3)

Introduction

Have you heard of pups, calves, cubs and kittens? If you have, you will know that these are the names given to some young animals.

What does a pup look like when it grows up? It grows into a bigger dog and looks like its parents. A lion cub looks like its parents, too. So do kittens and calves.

But when some animals and insects are born, they do not look anything like their parents. Some never even see their parents.

Tadpoles are young frogs that do not look anything like their parents when they are born. Caterpillars do not look anything like the butterfly that laid the eggs they hatched from. Locust nymphs also change as they grow.

When Caterpillars Grow

Do you know what a caterpillar turns into when it grows up? It will be a butterfly. Just as a tadpole does not look anything like a frog, a caterpillar does not look anything like a butterfly. A caterpillar looks like a little worm crawling on a leaf.

A female butterfly chooses very carefully where to lay her eggs.

Animals that Change as they Grow

A tadpole grows into a frog.

A caterpillar grows into a butterfly.

A nymph grows into a locust.

She does this because a caterpillar cannot fly from plant to plant looking for food. A caterpillar must hatch out of an egg on a plant that it can eat. It begins to eat as soon as it crawls out of the egg.

A sticky fluid on a butterfly's eggs helps hold the eggs on a leaf.

The little caterpillar, or larva of a butterfly, eats and eats. As it gets bigger, its skin becomes too tight for its growing body and splits. The caterpillar crawls out of its old skin and keeps eating. It grows even bigger and sheds its skin again. It does this until it is much bigger than it was when it hatched.

When a caterpillar grows to its full size, it fixes itself to a leaf by short threads of silk. It then becomes a pupa inside a firm case.
The case is called a chrysalis. While it is inside its chrysalis, the pupa changes completely. It turns into a butterfly.

When the pupa has become a butterfly, it breaks out of its chrysalis. It spreads its wings and flies away. The butterfly never eats leaves again. Instead, it feeds mostly on nectar. Like the frog, it has a new diet.

After a butterfly comes out of its chrysalis, it has to dry its crumpled wings before it can fly.

How a Caterpillar Grows

A butterfly lays eggs on a leaf.

A worm-like caterpillar hatches out of each egg.

The caterpillar turns into a pupa and grows inside a chrysalis.

A butterfly comes out of the chrysalis.

In time, the female butterflies look around for a plant where they will lay their eggs.

UNIT 23

Activities

A

Fact Finding

1. What is a tadpole?
2. What does a nymph turn into when it grows up?
3. What helps hold the butterfly's eggs on a leaf?
4. What is the firm case around a pupa called?
5. What creature comes out of a chrysalis?

B

Choose the word closest in meaning to the underlined word.

1. A caterpillar looks like a little worm **crawling** on a leaf.
   (a) walking (b) running
   (c) creeping (d) skipping
2. A sticky **fluid** on a butterfly's eggs helps hold the eggs on a leaf.
   (a) glue (b) liquid
   (c) cream (d) shell
3. The **larva** eats and eats.
   (a) mother (b) body
   (c) friend (d) young
4. The caterpillar **sheds** its skin again.
   (a) loses (b) grows
   (c) hurts (d) hides
5. While inside its chrysalis, the pupa changes **completely**.
   (a) somewhat (b) a little
   (c) totally (d) colour
6. When a butterfly comes out of the chrysalis, its wings are **crumpled**.
   (a) smooth (b) wrinkled
   (c) small (d) damaged

C

Choose the most suitable word to complete each sentence.

1. A female butterfly ________ very carefully where to lay her eggs. **(looks, decides, knows, sees)**
2. A caterpillar must ________ out of an egg on a plant that it can eat. **(dance, look, hop, break)**

3. As the caterpillar gets bigger its skin ________. **(wrinkles, sweats, rips, grows)**
4. It ________ itself to a leaf by short threads. **(sticks, pins, sews, darns)**
5. It then becomes a pupa inside a ________ case. **(weak, solid, flimsy, grey)**
6. Like the frog, the butterfly's ________ changes. **(wings, flight, food, nectar)**

D Choose the correct answer.

1. Young animals

(a) always look like their parents.

(b) never look like their parents.

(c) sometimes do not look like their parents.

(d) always look like their mothers.

2. The young of the locust is called

(a) a caterpillar. (b) a nymph.

(c) a tadpole. (d) a larva.

3. The female butterfly chooses very carefully where to lay her egg because

(a) the caterpillar needs very green leaves.

(b) the caterpillar needs a plant it can eat.

(c) she wants to hide her eggs.

(d) the caterpillar needs nectar.

4. A butterfly feeds mostly on

(a) pizza. (b) leaves.

(c) nectar. (d) honey.

5. What grows inside a chrysalis?

(a) A locust.

(b) A butterfly.

(c) A caterpillar.

(d) A lion.

E Grammar

There is the opposite of here, e.g. the little girl lives over there.
Their means belonging to them, e.g. they hung their coats on the pegs.
They're means they are, e.g. they're very quiet children.

Write there, their or they're.

1. Look at the frogs. ________ babies are called tadpoles.
2. I can see a locust over ________ .
3. Lion cubs look like ________ parents.
4. ________ like little worms crawling on leaves.
5. ________ is a lot of sticky fluid on a butterfly's eggs.
6. One thing to remember about caterpillars is that ________ always hungry.

F Summarise

How a caterpillar grows is summarised at the end of this piece. Only the important points are given. Summarise the introduction to the piece in your own words.

G Use Your Imagination

Imagine you are a beautiful butterfly. Write about how you changed from a wriggly caterpillar.

UNIT 24

The Scarlet Rose

Once upon a time in a faraway place, there lived a sea merchant and his three beautiful daughters. One summer's evening the merchant was preparing to go on a long voyage. He knew he would visit many wonderful countries and asked his daughters what gifts they would like him to bring back to them.

His first daughter, a tall graceful girl, asked for a golden tiara. The second daughter, who was beautiful but vain, asked for a mirror decorated with jewels. His third daughter, the kindest and most gentle of the three, asked only that her father return home safely and bring her a scarlet rose.

Early next morning, the merchant set sail. He visited many fine places and easily found a golden tiara and a mirror decorated with jewels. However, his heart was heavy as he returned home because he had been unable to find a scarlet rose for his favourite daughter.

When the ship landed, the merchant set off for home on foot. However, he was so distracted that he took a wrong turning and found himself in an enchanted wood. Deep in the wood, the merchant discovered a palace with a beautiful shrub growing at the door. As he came closer, the merchant realised that the red flower on the shrub was a scarlet rose. He was overjoyed to have found, at last, what he had been searching for. He bent down and picked the rose.

Suddenly he heard a great roar. A hideous beast appeared. The beast was very angry. He asked the merchant why he had stolen the rose.

The merchant told the beast how he had travelled far and wide but had failed to find a scarlet rose for his youngest daughter. The beast told the merchant that he could keep the rose, but only if one of his daughters returned to live forever in the beast's enchanted palace.

When he reached home, the merchant told his daughters what had happened. The youngest daughter, Ana, said that she would go and live with the beast. Her family were afraid for her and did not want her to leave, but she was determined to keep her father's promise.

Ana lived very happily in the beast's palace for a time. The beast would not allow her see him but he made sure his servants took good care of her. The servants showed her much kindness. Ana began to grow fond of the beast. One day she asked the beast to show himself to her. He did as she asked, but just as he feared, she screamed in terror when she saw him. This made the beast very sad.

One night Ana dreamed that her father was very ill. She asked the beast if she could return home to be with him. The beast feared he might lose Ana forever. He agreed that she could go home, but only if she promised to return within three days. Ana promised.

When he saw his daughter, the merchant started to recover quickly. He had missed her so much. When he was feeling stronger, Ana told him about her promise to the beast and prepared to leave home. Her sisters did not want her to return to the beast and they changed the time on the clocks.

Ana arrived at the palace four days after she had left. As she approached the palace door, Ana saw the beast lying on the ground beside the shrub. He had a scarlet rose on his chest. His eyes were closed. Ana believed he was dead but she bent down over him hoping to hear a breath. Heartbroken, she started to cry. Her tears fell on the beast and broke an evil spell. Her beloved beast awoke. Before Ana's eyes, he slowly turned into a handsome prince and they lived together happily ever after.

UNIT 24 Activities

A Fact Finding

1. How many daughters did the merchant have?
2. Which gifts were easy to find?
3. Where did the merchant find the scarlet rose?
4. What promise did Ana make the beast?
5. Where did Ana find the beast when she returned to the palace?

B Choose the word closest in meaning to the underlined word.

1. Once upon a time in a **faraway** place there lived a sea merchant.
   (a) nearby (b) distant
   (c) close (d) remote
2. The merchant was **preparing** to go on a long voyage.
   (a) about (b) able
   (c) planning (d) ready
3. He was in an **enchanted** wood.
   (a) magical (b) dark
   (c) scary (d) interesting
4. A **hideous** beast appeared.
   (a) handsome (b) shy
   (c) ugly (d) pretty
5. Ana was **determined** to keep her father's promise.
   (a) happy to (b) intent on
   (c) afraid to (d) nervous about
6. When he saw his daughter, the merchant started to **recover**.
   (a) worsen (b) grow
   (c) sing (d) improve

C Choose the most suitable word to complete each sentence.

1. The merchant was preparing to go on a long ________. **(sail, journey, run, walk)**
2. He had been unable to find a scarlet rose for his ________ daughter. **(lovely, tall, beautiful, best-loved)**
3. Deep in the wood, the merchant ________ a palace. **(built, found, destroyed, entered)**
4. He was ________ to have found at last what he had been searching for. **(delighted, amazed, stunned, happy)**
5. Ana began to ________ the beast. **(hate, love, despise, like)**
6. As she ________ the door, Ana saw the beast on the ground. **(unlocked, opened, approached, pushed)**

D

Choose the correct answer.

1. **The second daughter asked for a mirror because**
   (a) she like shiny things.
   (b) she was vain.
   (c) she did not have one.
   (d) she wanted to look at her hair.
2. **Where did the merchant find the rose?**
   (a) Beside the palace drawbridge.
   (b) Beside the palace door.
   (c) Beside the palace window.
   (d) Beside the palace gate.
3. **The beast was angry because**
   (a) the merchant had picked the rose.
   (b) the merchant had smelt the rose.
   (c) the merchant had seen the rose.
   (d) the merchant had touched the rose.
4. **The beast would not allow Ana see him, for fear she would**
   (a) fall in love with him.
   (b) be afraid of him.
   (c) beg him to go home.
   (d) cry.
5. **What did Ana's sisters do to delay her return to the palace?**
   (a) They changed the calendar.
   (b) They hid her clothes.
   (c) They locked her in her room.
   (d) They changed the time on the clocks.

E

Grammar

Fill the blanks with suitable adjectives.

1. The sea merchant had three ________ daughters.
2. One ________ summer's evening, he was getting ready to go on a ________ voyage.
3. He easily found the ________ tiara but not the ________ rose.
4. Ana went to live in the ________ beast's ________ palace.
5. When he saw his ________ daughter, the ________ merchant recovered quickly.
6. Ana's ________ beast awoke and turned into a ________ prince.

F

Character Description

Ana is described as being "the kindest and most gentle of the three girls". Read the story and find examples of Ana's kindness and gentleness.

G

Use Your Imagination

Write the story of how the spell was cast on the handsome prince, changing him into a hideous beast.

UNIT 25 Dad, Sam & Blacky

Dad, Sam and Blacky were walking through the countryside on their way to the village market. The sky was blue with very few clouds and the birds were singing a happy chorus in the trees.

"Ah, this is the life, Dad," said Sam.

"It really is, Sam," said the man. "Look at Blacky. He looks cheerful too."

"Is that right, Blacky?" Sam asked playfully.

Blacky snorted merrily and twitched his ears and tail.

The three of them walked happily along until they came to a garden. Two children were swinging on a gate.

"What is the point of having a horse and not riding it?" asked one of the children.

Sam, his dad and Blacky had always walked everywhere together. Now, however, Sam and his dad thought about what the child had asked and wondered if maybe they looked silly.

"Maybe you should get up on Blacky's back, Sam," said his dad.

"Okay," said Sam and up he got.

They continued on their journey. Looking up, Sam noticed that clouds were starting to gather. He really hoped nothing would spoil this perfect day. Just then the trio passed a farmer and his wife. They were working hard pitching hay into a trailer.

The farmer turned to his wife and said, "Did you see that lazy child letting his poor father walk while he sits there on the horse's back?"

"Shocking!" said his wife, shaking her head. "What is the world coming to?"

Sam knew that his dad was happy for him to ride the horse but he wanted people to see that he had respect for his father. He swapped places with his dad and they hurried on.

Next they passed a field, where a man and a woman were rounding up their cows for milking.

"Oh, that poor little boy," said the woman. "He is forced to walk while his father rides along at his leisure."

"That's very sad," said the man with a tear in his eye. "It's a crying shame."

Sam and his dad were very puzzled. They were not sure who should ride the horse so they stopped by the side of the road to think. The sun had disappeared behind the clouds and it started to rain. They were quite close to the village so they decided that they would both ride the horse the rest of the way. Sam got back on the horse and offered his hand to his father.

Just as they both were ready to ride on, a cart came along and slowed down beside them. An angry-looking driver spoke to them.

"You are too heavy for that horse!" he said "Why should that animal suffer, just because you are too lazy to walk?"

He drove away, leaving Sam and his dad more confused than ever. Just then a loud crack of thunder sounded and a heavy shower of rain began to fall.

"I think we should carry Blacky the rest of the way," said Sam's dad. "It's the only thing we haven't tried yet."

Blacky neighed a few times with surprise as they lifted him up and stumbled onwards.

When they reached the village, Sam and his dad were soaked and exhausted. Blacky's tail was dripping wet and it kept swinging into Sam's face, causing him to grumble.

"Nearly there, son, nearly there," his dad called out.

They put Blacky down and realised that a group of onlookers were watching them in amazement.

"Have you ever seen anything so ridiculous?" said one.

"There's a first time for everything," said another.

A wise old woman was standing apart from the crowd. She asked Sam and his dad why they were carrying the horse. They told her about all the people they had met along the way.

"Ah," she said. "So you tried to please everybody!"

"Yes," replied Sam's dad.

"That's where you went wrong," the old woman responded. "It is impossible to please everybody. If you try, you usually end up pleasing nobody!"

Sam, his dad and Blacky walked home side by side, thinking about what the woman had said. They had learned a valuable lesson.

UNIT 25

Activities

A Fact Finding

1. Where were Dad, Sam and Blacky going?
2. What were the farmer and his wife doing?
3. Why did Sam swap places with his dad?
4. Why were the crowd watching Sam and his dad in amazement?
5. Who was standing apart from the crowd?

B Choose the word closest in meaning to the underlined word.

1. Blacky looks **cheerful** too.
   (a) sad (b) excited
   (c) bored (d) happy
2. Blacky **twitched** his ears.
   (a) dropped (b) jerked
   (c) lifted (d) curled
3. Sam really hoped nothing would **spoil** his perfect day.
   (a) ruin (b) wet
   (c) shorten (d) lengthen
4. He **swapped** places with his dad.
   (a) passed (b) drove
   (c) changed (d) travelled
5. Sam was very **puzzled**.
   (a) content (b) confused
   (c) concerned (d) confined
6. When they reached the village, they were soaked and **exhausted**.
   (a) wet (b) angry
   (c) sodden (d) tired

C Choose the most suitable word to complete each sentence.

1. The children could not ________ why Sam and his dad were not riding the horse. **(ask, say, understand, wonder)**
2. The farmer and his wife were ________ hay into a trailer. **(putting, tossing, turning, burning)**
3. Sam wanted people to see he had ________ for his father. **(regard, love, pity, concern)**
4. Blacky's tail was swinging into Sam's face causing him to ________. **(cry, yell, complain, mutter)**
5. "Have you ever seen anything so ________," one of the onlookers said. **(funny, strange, awful, silly)**
6. Sam and his dad learned a ________ lesson. **(expensive, useful, useless, stupid)**

D

Choose the correct answer.

1. When Sam said, "This is the life," he meant

(a) I am tired. (b) I am happy.

(c) I am bored. (d) I am weary.

2. For whom did the woman in the field feel sorry?

(a) Sam. (b) Blacky.

(c) Sam's dad. (d) Herself.

3. Why did Sam and his dad decide they would both ride Blacky?

(a) They were tired.

(b) Blacky told them to.

(c) They would get to the village quicker.

(d) They did not know what else to do.

4. Where was the wise old woman standing?

(a) In the crowd.

(b) Beside the crowd.

(c) Apart from the crowd.

(d) On the market stall.

5. What was the valuable lesson Sam and his dad learned?

(a) You cannot please most people.

(b) You cannot please yourself.

(c) You cannot please children.

(d) You cannot please everybody.

E

Grammar

Write these words in alphabetical order.

1. Sam, dad, Blacky, horse, market.
2. Children, farmer, woman, man, gate.
3. Twitched, tail, two, three, together.
4. Shocking, swopped, sorry, slowed, suffered.
5. Forced, father, walk, ride, rain.
6. Watching, looking, wise, please, lesson.

F

Summarise

Write a short piece telling the wise old woman about all the people Dad and Sam met and all the advice they were given.

G

Explore the Text

In this story Sam and his dad learned a very valuable lesson. The little fir tree and Amy in "The Dreamer" both learned valuable lessons.
Read both these stories again. They are in Unit 15 and Unit 21. Write the lesson learned by these characters in your own words.

UNIT 26

Two Games to Make and Play

Around the world children have one thing in common. They love to play games. In some parts of the world families do not have enough money to buy games and so the children become good at making them out of whatever they can find. You too can have fun doing this. Before starting the games here, make sure you read the instructions, gather the materials you need and understand how the scoring works. Enjoy!

Game One – Jack Stones

Games with Jacks are played in many countries all over the world. Children in India play a game called Pacheta. It is a game for two players, played outdoors on dry ground using small stones. It is very similar to Jack Stones.

Making the game:

1. Clean the stones well. Draw and paint a different shape on each stone.
2. Varnish each stone and leave to dry.

Make sure all the stones are fully dry before you use them in the game.

Playing the game:

1. Hold the stones in the palm of your hand. Carefully toss them in the air.
2. Catch the stones on the back of your hand as they fall. If you keep your fingers together, the stones won't fall through.
3. Throw the stones in the air again, catching them in the palm of your hand.

The person who has caught the most stones goes first.

4. Place all the stones on the ground. Throw one stone in the air and before you catch it again, pick one stone from the ground with the same hand. Keep doing this until you have picked up all the stones, one at a time.

5. Place all the stones on the ground again. Throw one stone in the air and before you catch it pick up two stones with the same hand. Keep doing this until you have picked up all the stones two at a time.
6. Repeat twice more, picking up three stones first, then four. If you miss, or drop a stone, the other player has a turn. When it's your turn again, you start from where you left off.

Another version of this is to place the stones on the ground. Make an arch on the ground with your thumb and first finger. Throw a stone up and with the same hand tap one stone through the arch before catching the stone. Continue until all the stones are tapped through, one by one. Then try tapping pairs, threes and fours through.

To finish the game, throw one stone in the air and gather up all the other stones with the same hand before catching the one you threw!

Game Two – Shell Jacks

This is a great game for two people to play on the beach.

Playing the game:

1. Place five shells in a hole in the sand.
2. Throw a shell in the air. Using the same hand, scoop all the shells out of the hole before catching the shell you threw.
3. If you don't catch the thrown shell or if you leave any shells in the hole, it is your friend's turn.
4. When you have scooped up all five shells, place six shells in the hole. Try to beat your own score each time. The aim of this game is to scoop up 19 shells before catching the shell you have thrown.

UNIT 26

Activities

A Fact Finding

1. What must you do before you start making the games?
2. In which country do children play Pacheta?
3. How many stones do you need for the game Jack Stones?
4. Where is the best place to play Shell Jacks?
5. What is the aim of Shell Jacks?

B Choose the word closest in meaning to the underlined word.

1. Read the **instructions** carefully before you make the games.
   (a) story (b) directions
   (c) box (d) leaflet
2. Pacheta is **similar to** Jack Stones.
   (a) like (b) different to
   (c) unlike (d) the same as
3. Make sure all the stones are **fully** dry before using them.
   (a) slightly (b) somewhat
   (c) fairly (d) completely
4. Carefully **toss** the stones in the air.
   (a) bat (b) throw
   (c) blow (d) hit
5. Using the same hand, **scoop** all the shells out of the hole.
   (a) toss (b) spoon
   (c) lift (d) ease
6. The **aim** of this game is to scoop up 19 shells.
   (a) fun (b) difficulty
   (c) trouble (d) purpose

C Choose the most suitable word to complete each sentence.

1. Children ________ playing games. **(hate, fear, enjoy, dread)**
2. Remember to gather all the ________ you need before starting to make the game. **(children, money, people, materials)**
3. When the stones are clean, draw and paint a ________ shape on each one. **(new, silly, matching, similar)**
4. Another ________ of playing Jack Stones starts with the stones on the ground. **(shape, difficulty, way, memory)**
5. Make a ________ on the ground with your thumb and first finger. **(square, curve, line, triangle)**
6. ________ playing the game until all the stones are tapped through. **(stop, start, begin, keep)**

D

Choose the correct answer.

1. **Where is the Indian game of Pacheta played?**
   (a) Outdoors on sandy ground.
   (b) Outdoors on grassy ground.
   (c) Outdoors on dry ground.
   (d) Outdoors on wet ground.
2. **Which of the following do you not need to make Jack Stones?**
   (a) Varnish. (b) Paint.
   (c) A pencil. (d) Shells.
3. **In Jack Stones, where do you catch the stones the first time they fall?**
   (a) In the palm of your hand.
   (b) On the back of your hand.
   (c) On your elbow.
   (d) In your fist.
4. **In Shell Jacks, where do you place the shells?**
   (a) In a bucket.
   (b) On a spade.
   (c) In a hole in the sand.
   (d) In a hole in the sea.
5. **What do you try to beat each time you play Shell Jacks?**
   (a) Your own score.
   (b) Your friend's score.
   (c) Your Dad's score.
   (d) Your Mum's score.

E

Grammar

Revision: Too, two and to; its and it's.

Choose the correct word to finish each sentence.

1. Children all over the world love ________ play games. **(too, two, to)**
2. Shell Jacks is a great game for ________ people to play on the beach. **(too, two, to)**
3. Throw one stone in the air and pick up ________ stones with the same hand. **(too, two, to)**
4. ________ important to read the instructions first. **(Its, It's)**
5. Clean the stone and draw a shape on ________ surface. **(its, it's)**
6. When ________ your turn again, you start from where you left off. **(its, it's)**

F

Summarise

Read the instructions for playing Shell Jacks. Write a short summary in your own words.

G

Explore the Text

This piece of writing gives instructions. Each instruction is numbered and is clearly explained. It is similar to writing a list. Read the second version of Jack Stones and write it in your own words. Number and explain each instruction clearly.

UNIT 27 The Frog Prince

Once upon a time there lived a beautiful princess. She was the youngest and most beautiful of all the king's daughters. She was so lovely that even the sun itself smiled when she came out to play.

One fine day the princess put on her cloak and shoes and went outside. She carried a little golden ball. She loved throwing the ball high up into the air and catching it as it fell. She skipped through the forest playing happily with her golden ball.

After a while the princess arrived at a stream which flowed through the forest. She saw how the sun's rays shone through the trees and made beautiful patterns on the surface of the water. She watched the patterns for a while and then started to play with the golden ball again. She tossed the ball as high as she could into the air. However, as it came down the sun shone in her eyes and she missed it. The ball hit a rock, bounced into the stream and sank to the bottom. The princess lay down beside the stream and tried to find the ball but she could not see it anywhere. She was very upset.

Suddenly she heard a low, croaky voice. The voice asked her what was the matter. The princess looked up but could not see anybody. A small, green frog jumped up onto a rock beside her.

"It was I who spoke," he said. "Why are you sad?"

"I am sad because my little, golden ball bounced into this stream and is now lost forever," replied the princess.

"If you make me three promises I will swim to the bottom of the stream and get your ball," the frog croaked.

"What are the three promises?" asked the princess.

"You must promise to be my friend, let me share your food and drink and let me sleep in your little bed," the frog croaked.

The princess promised. The frog hopped off the rock and landed in the water with a loud splash. He disappeared under the surface and within a few minutes was back with the ball. The princess was thrilled. She took the ball and skipped home happily. She forgot all about the three promises she had made to the frog.

That evening the princess was having tea with her family. Suddenly she heard a loud, croaking noise at the window. She remembered her three promises to the frog and began to feel afraid. The king noticed that his daughter looked upset and asked her what was wrong. She told him about the frog and the three promises she had made.

"Your promise is your word, my little daughter," the king said. "You must always keep your word. This frog will be our guest. Go and bring him to our table."

The princess walked reluctantly towards the window and invited the frog to join them. The frog hopped onto the table and began to eat from her plate. He then drank from her cup. The princess shuddered.

When the meal was over, she tried to slip away unnoticed. The frog hopped after her. The king saw what was happening.

"Remember your last promise, princess. You must bring the frog to your room," he said.

The princess picked up the frog very carefully. She held him as far away from her as possible. She placed him on the floor in the corner of her room.

"You shall sleep there," she said.

"Oh no, I shall sleep in your bed," the frog croaked.

Before the princess could say a word the frog had hopped into her little bed and snuggled down under the covers. Close to tears, the princess got into bed. She stayed as close as she could to her own side. Suddenly the little, green frog started to change. He changed into a very handsome prince.

"An evil witch cast a spell on me," he said. "Your kindness and care has broken the spell. I am forever grateful to you."

The princess was amazed. She and the prince became the best of friends and spent many happy days playing together.

UNIT 27

Activities

A

Fact Finding

1. What game did the princess like to play with her golden ball?
2. What made beautiful patterns on the surface of the water?
3. Why was the princess crying?
4. What promise did the princess make to the frog?
5. When the frog hopped onto the table, what did he start to do?

B

Choose the word closest in meaning to the underlined word.

1. The sun's rays made beautiful patterns on the **surface** of the water.
   (a) bottom (b) top
   (c) side (d) edge
2. She **tossed** the ball as high as she could into the air.
   (a) bounced (b) kicked
   (c) hit (d) threw
3. The princess was **thrilled**.
   (a) delighted (b) bored
   (c) dismayed (d) shocked
4. The princess **shuddered**.
   (a) laughed (b) shouted
   (c) trembled (d) fainted
5. When the meal was over, she tried to slip away **unnoticed**.
   (a) quietly (b) unseen
   (c) quickly (d) outside
6. "I am forever **grateful** to you," the handsome prince said.
   (a) married (b) joined
   (c) friendly (d) thankful

C

Choose the most suitable word to complete each sentence.

1. One ________ day, the princess put on her cloak and went outside. **(wet, windy, pleasant, cold)**
2. She watched the patterns for a ________. **(day, time, week, hour)**
3. "The frog will be our ________," said the king. **(friend, pet, visitor, mascot)**
4. The princess walked ________ to the window. **(quickly, awkwardly, happily, slowly)**
5. The frog ________ down under the covers. **(nestled, hopped, jumped, shot)**
6. He changed into a very ________ prince. **(ugly, good-looking, pretty, tall)**

D

Choose the correct answer.

1. Why did the sun smile when the princess came out to play?

(a) Because she was so sad.

(b) Because she was so lovely.

(c) Because she was so happy.

(d) Because she was so bright.

2. Why did the princess not catch the ball?

(a) It got stuck in a tree.

(b) It got lost in the shadows.

(c) She was blinded by the sun.

(d) The frog caught it.

3. When did the princess remember the three promises she had made to the frog?

(a) At breakfast with her family.

(b) At dinner with her family.

(c) At lunch with her family.

(d) At tea with her family.

4. When the king said, "Your promise is your word," he meant

(a) You must keep your promise.

(b) You must forget your promise.

(c) You must make another promise

(d) You should never make a promise.

5. Who had cast the spell on the frog?

(a) An evil wizard.

(b) An exciting witch.

(c) An evil witch.

(d) An evil warlock.

E

Grammar

Complete each sentence using a suitable verb.

1. She loved ________ the ball up and ________ it as it fell.

2. The ball ________ a rock and ________ into the stream.

3. I will ________ to the bottom of the stream and ________ your ball.

4. The princess ________ the ball and ________ home happily.

5. The princess ________ towards the window and ________ the frog in.

6. The princess and the prince ________ many happy days ________ .

F

Character Description

The frog tells the princess that her kindness and care broke the spell. Do you think the princess was kind and caring?
Write a short paragraph explaining your answer.

G

Explore the Text

"The Frog Prince" is a fairy tale. So is "The Scarlet Rose" in Unit 24. Read both stories again. What do they have in common? Make a list.

UNIT 28

Clever Rosa

Rosa lived on a small farm with her mother and father. One day her father decided to plant a crop of cassava. (Cassava is a plant that grows in South America.) The root of the cassava is used to make meal with which cassava cakes can be baked. Rosa and her family loved to eat these cakes with eggs and cheese. The family worked together to clear a piece of land. They then prepared the soil and planted the tiny seeds. Throughout the seasons, Rosa helped to tend the crop and before long it was time for it to be harvested.

One morning, before the sun was too high in the sky, Rosa walked with her father to the field to start working. To their dismay, they discovered that most of the roots had been pulled out and chewed by wild animals. They could not believe their eyes! They returned home feeling very annoyed and Rosa's father told his wife what had happened. The couple decided that the man would return to the field the next day. He would dig a hole and make a trap to capture the animals that were digging up the cassava roots.

While the farmer was digging the hole, he heard a noise from a tree nearby. He looked up and saw a nasty troll standing beside him. He became afraid.

"Why are you digging that hole?" the troll asked.

"To capture the animals that are stealing our cassava plants," the farmer replied.

The troll offered to help on condition that the farmer would share with him any animals trapped in the pit. The farmer, who was scared that the troll might hurt him, agreed.

"You can have the male animals and I will keep the female ones," the troll growled as they worked together, finishing the trap.

The following morning the farmer returned to the field to see if any animals had fallen into the trap. To his delight he discovered a male buffalo in the pit. He took it home. Each day male animals such as antelope and wild pigs fell into the pit. The farmer was thrilled.

"You made a bad choice," he said to the troll. "Did you not know that it's mostly male animals that hunt for food?"

The farmer's wife was delighted with all the meat they now had in storage but she still longed for some cassava cake. One evening she decided to go to the farm herself to see if she could get even a small piece of the root. All she wanted was enough to make one small cake.

She was gone for a while and Rosa started to miss her.

"Will Mama be back soon?" she asked her father.

It was a lovely warm evening, so they decided to walk to the farm and meet her there. As they got near the farm, they heard the troll shouting loudly.

"Hooray, hooray, I've got an animal today!"

The farmer and his daughter ran to the pit and looked in. They could not believe their eyes. The farmer's wife was in the trap!

"This is my wife," the farmer shouted at the troll. "You cannot keep her!"

The pair started arguing and the troll became very angry. At last Rosa, who had been watching everything and saying nothing, spoke.

"You must keep your word, Father," she said. "We have had plenty of animals from the trap and the troll has had none. This one is his."

There was silence. Rosa's father could not believe his ears.

"B…b…but this is your beloved mother," he stammered.

"You have a clever daughter," the troll shouted with glee, and he jumped into the pit to claim his prize.

Rosa suddenly shouted and pointed to the troll. "Look, Father, there is a male animal in the pit and it is yours!"

The farmer smiled.

"You are right, troll," he said, "my daughter is indeed a clever girl and you are now mine!"

The troll was livid. He had been tricked by a young girl! He came to an agreement with the farmer. The farmer would let the troll go free if the troll freed the farmer's wife. Rosa and her parents laughed all the way home. Her mother and father were very proud of their clever daughter.

UNIT 28

Activities

A Fact Finding

1. What did Rosa and her parents like to eat with the cassava cakes?
2. What did Rosa and her father discover when they went to harvest the cassava?
3. Who did the farmer meet when he was getting the trap ready?
4. What did Rosa and her father do when her mother had not returned home?
5. Why was the troll livid?

B Choose the word closest in meaning to the underlined word.

1. **Throughout** the seasons, Rosa helped to tend the cassava crop.
   (a) after (b) during
   (c) before (d) following
2. To their **dismay**, they discovered that the crop had been eaten!
   (a) joy (b) surprise
   (c) pleasure (d) disappointment
3. There was a male buffalo in the **pit**.
   (a) trap (b) field
   (c) leaves (d) trees
4. They were delighted with all the meat they now had in **in storage**.
   (a) eaten (b) frozen
   (c) stored (d) wasted
5. The pair started **arguing**.
   (a) laughing (b) quarrelling
   (c) playing (d) singing
6. The troll was **livid**.
   (a) cross (b) sad
   (c) upset (d) furious

C Choose the most suitable word to complete each sentence.

1. Before long it was time for the crop to be ________. **(sown, watered, picked, planted)**
2. He looked up and saw a ________ troll standing beside him. **(nice, horrible, tiny, huge)**
3. She still ________ some cassava cake. **(desired, hated, loved, waited)**
4. "B…b…but this is your beloved mother," he ________. **(shouted, said, sang, stuttered)**
5. "You have a clever daughter," the troll shouted with ________. **(annoyance, joy, pride, hatred)**
6. Rosa's parents were very ________ their daughter. **(annoyed with, afraid of, pleased with, ashamed of)**

D

Choose the correct answer.

1. What can be baked from the roots of the cassava plant?

(a) Cassava buns.

(b) Cassava cake.

(c) Cassava tart.

(d) Cassava tea.

2. What had pulled out and chewed most of the roots?

(a) The troll. (b) Tame animals.

(c) Wild animals. (d) The birds.

3. What deal did the troll make with the farmer?

(a) They would share the trapped animals equally.

(b) The troll would eat the fat animals.

(c) The troll would keep the male animals.

(d) The troll would keep the female animals.

4. Why did the troll and the farmer start arguing?

(a) The troll did not want to keep the farmer's wife.

(b) The troll wanted to keep the farmer's wife.

(c) The farmer wanted the troll to eat cassava.

(d) The troll wanted to swap the farmer's wife for Rosa.

5. Why was the troll livid?

(a) He had been tricked.

(b) He was hungry.

(c) He was starving.

(d) He was trapped in the pit.

E

Grammar

Write the plural of the underlined words.

1. The **girl** walked to the **field** with her **father**.
2. A wild **fox** had pulled out the **root** of the cassava **plant**.
3. They had planted **potato**, **tomato** and **cabbage**.
4. A male **buffalo**, **pig** and **antelope** fell into the **trap**.
5. The wife's **wish** was for a **dish** of cassava **cake**.
6. "You have a clever **daughter**," the **troll** shouted as he jumped in to collect his **prize**.

F

Summarise

Rosa solved the problem when her mother got caught in the trap. Read the paragraph which explains the trick she played and write it in your own words.

G

Use Your Imagination

Imagine you are the troll. Give yourself a name. Where do you live? Write the conversation you have with your family when you return home, yet again, with no food.

UNIT 29

The Toy Catalogue

BUDDA SPECIAL OFFERS FOR ONE WEEK ONLY

When the sun shines, everyone wants to be outside. Here at Budda we have a wonderful selection of outdoor toys for all ages. While the children are having fun, the adults can sit back and relax!

Remember … Slap on the sun cream!

€200.00

Play Centre

Why not try our play centre, with two swings, a climbing rope and a see-saw? The slide can be purchased on its own and attached easily. All wood is weather treated.

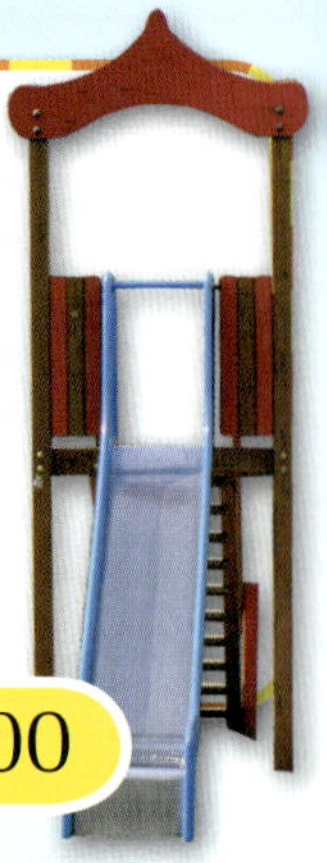

Slide attachment €100.00

Trampolines

Jumping on a trampoline is lots of fun, for adults and children alike. It is a great form of exercise and improves balance and rhythm for young children. Here at Budda we have trampolines to suit all ages and all garden sizes.

Toddler Trampolines come with extra padding and full safety nets. **€100.00**

8ft Trampolines come with safety net. **€150.00**

10ft Trampolines come with safety net. **€230.00**

13ft Trampolines come with safety net and ladder. **€300.00**

PECIAL OFFER
FOR ONE WEEK ONLY!
Free electric pump worth €25.00 with every family pool bought.

Family Pool

Large, metal-framed pool for the whole family.
Ideal for that "quick dip" when the sun is too hot!
Needs to be placed on flat ground.
Price includes pool cover and ladder.

€269.00

Great savings in our Bike Department!

Bikes

We have a large selection of bikes in our store.

24 inch mountain bike with steel frame. Comes with 21 speeds, 18 gears, v-brakes and alloy rimmed wheels.

Was €99.00, now only €89.00

20 inch girl's bike with lightweight frame, includes front and rear alloy wheels and brakes. **Was €120.00, now only €99.00**

Safety First

Always wear a helmet when using your scooter or bike.
Wear your helmet flat on your head, not tilted back at an angle
Make sure your helmet fits snugly and that the chin straps fit securely
Check your helmet often for cracks or broken buckles.

Come in-store to see our huge selection of outdoor games, balls, skipping ropes and skateboards

UNIT 29 Activities

A Fact Finding

1. For how long will the special offers at Budda last?
2. What should you remember to put on before going out to play?
3. What do you get with the toddler trampolines?
4. Where does the family pool need to be placed?
5. Which bike has 21 speeds?

B Choose the word closest in meaning to the underlined word.

1. Here at Budda, we have a wonderful **selection** of toys.
   (a) box (b) shelf (c) net (d) choice
2. The slide can be **purchased** on its own.
   (a) lost (b) bought
   (c) stolen (d) broken
3. Jumping on a trampoline is a great **form** of exercise.
   (a) type (b) shape
   (c) outline (d) start
4. Follow a few **simple** rules.
   (a) difficult (b) strange
   (c) odd (d) easy
5. The pool should be **placed** on flat ground.
   (a) put (b) built
   (c) filled (d) painted
6. Make sure the chin straps of your helmet fit **securely**.
   (a) safely (b) tightly
   (c) loosely (d) strictly

C Choose the most suitable word to complete each sentence.

1. Our climbing frames and swings _________ children lots of healthy activity. **(give, lose, find, bounce)**
2. The slide can be _________ easily to our climbing frames. **(leaned, joined, broken, slid)**
3. _________ on a trampoline is lots of fun. **(Bouncing, Sitting, Singing, Sleeping)**
4. Toddler Trampolines come with _________ padding. **(no, some, more, thin)**
5. Our family pool is a _________, metal-framed pool for the whole family. **(small, tiny, huge, strong)**
6. Always have your bicycle helmet _________ on your head. **(tipped, straight, twisted, tilted)**

D

Choose the correct answer.

1. **Jumping on a trampoline**
   (a) destroys balance and rhythm.
   (b) damages balance and rhythm.
   (c) helps balance and rhythm.
   (d) hinders balance and rhythm.
2. **What should you always have on a trampoline?**
   (a) A child. (b) A safety net.
   (c) A cover. (d) A ladder.
3. **What comes free with every family pool purchased?**
   (a) An electric wire.
   (b) An electric fan.
   (c) An electric drier.
   (d) An electric pump.
4. **In which department will you get "Great Savings"?**
   (a) The Pool Department.
   (b) The Bike Department.
   (c) The Trampoline Department.
   (d) The Slide Department.
5. **For €89.00 you can buy**
   (a) a 24 inch mountain bike.
   (b) a 20 inch girl's bike.
   (c) a 24 inch boy's bike.
   (d) a 20 inch mountain bike.

E

Grammar

Revision: No and know; there, their and they're.

Choose the correct word to finish each sentence.

1. We _________ the special offers last for only one week. **(no, know)**
2. There are _________ climbing frames for sale in Budda. **(no, know)**
3. _________ wrestling and _________ somersaults on the trampoline. **(no, know)**
4. Place the trampoline over _________, well away from trees and buildings. **(there, their, they're)**
5. The lightweight frames mean _________ easier to lift. **(there, their, they're)**
6. Budda say that _________ huge selection of outdoor games can be seen in-store. **(there, their, they're)**

F

Summarise

Write a short summary of the "wonderful selection of outdoor toys" which can be bought at Budda.

G

Use Your Imagination

This toy catalogue could be called a summer toy catalogue. Design your own Christmas toy catalogue.

UNIT 30 A Lesson in Sharing

A farmer travelled from his tiny village in China to the market in the nearest large town. He had worked very hard for many months feeding, watering and caring for the peach trees he grew in his small garden. His work had paid off, for he now had a large crop of beautiful, sweet peaches to sell and he was determined to get a really good price for them!

He arrived in the marketplace just as the sun rose. Being so early, he was able to choose one of the best sites to park his barrow. He sat in the shade on a small stool and waited for the people to arrive. On entering the marketplace, the first thing people saw were the beautiful, golden peaches. The peaches were juicy and sweet and the people crowded around the barrow to buy them. The farmer was overjoyed. His purse was filling up with coins and it was still early in the day. He had many more peaches to sell.

Just before noon, a monk approached the farmer and asked him for a peach.

"I have no money and cannot pay you," said the monk.

"Then I shall not give you a peach," the farmer replied. "If I were to give you a free peach then I would have to do the same for every beggar. I could not make money like that!"

The monk returned many times, but the farmer refused each time. An old man who was sitting nearby had observed what was happening. He walked up to the farmer's barrow and bought a peach. He then handed it to the monk.

The monk thanked the man for his kindness. By now a crowd had gathered. They were amazed at how mean the farmer was.

"He is so greedy!" one man shouted.

"Does he not know this monk has no land, no house and no money?" another man wondered.

"How could he refuse to give this poor man one peach?" a woman asked.

"You have so many peaches in your barrow and so much money in your purse," the monk said, "it is very sad you could not find it in your heart to share with a hungry man."

The monk turned to the crowd that had gathered.

"I would like to thank you all for your kindness to me," he said. "I will share my peaches with you."

People looked at each other. They could not understand why this man had asked for a peach if he already had enough peaches to share with them. They wondered where the peaches were, because the monk had nothing with him.

They watched the monk as he slowly ate the peach. He chewed slowly, enjoying the taste of each morsel and allowing the juice to trickle down his throat. When he was finished he took the peach stone and planted it in the ground.

"Could I have some water please?" he asked the waiting crowd.

An old woman passed him a cup of water, which he poured on the soil. Within a few minutes a shoot appeared. The shoot grew taller. Leaves appeared, small ones at first and then bigger ones.

The seed soon became a tall tree and nestling among its leaves were several ripe, golden peaches. The people could not believe their eyes. The monk invited each person to come and pick a peach.

"We have never tasted peaches so delicious and sweet!" they cried.

Then, before their eyes, the monk chopped down the tree, lifted it up and left the market place.

The farmer had watched it all. He became angry. He knew that no more people would buy his peaches that day. He decided to go home but when he turned to put his stool in the barrow, he saw that it was empty. All his peaches had gone! He was furious!

"I shall follow that monk and demand payment for my peaches," he thought.

As he bent to push his barrow, he realized one of the handles was missing! By now the farmer was livid. He raced out of the market place, but he could not see the monk. He kept running, hoping to find him, but he had no luck. All he found was the trunk of the peach tree and as he lifted it off the ground it changed into the handle of his barrow!

UNIT 30

Activities

A

Fact Finding

1. What was the farmer selling in the market?
2. Who asked the farmer for a free peach?
3. What did the monk do when he had finished eating the peach?
4. Why was the farmer angry?
5. When the farmer turned to put his stool in his barrow, what did he see?

B

Choose the word closest in meaning to the underlined word.

1. He was able to **choose** one of the best sites.
   (a) lose (b) pick
   (c) paint (d) clutter

2. The farmer was **overjoyed**.
   (a) thrilled (b) annoyed
   (c) angry (d) dismayed
3. An old man had **observed** what was happening.
   (a) hidden (b) denied
   (c) watched (d) ignored
4. He enjoyed each **morsel**.
   (a) peach (b) trickle
   (c) one (d) piece
5. Nestled among its leaves, were several **ripe** peaches.
   (a) rotten (b) mature
   (c) tasty (d) bad
6. "We have never tasted peaches so **delicious** and sweet," they said.
   (a) ripe (b) sugary
   (c) tasty (d) juicy

C

Choose the most suitable word to complete each sentence.

1. Being so early, he was able to choose one of the best __________ to park his barrow. **(trailers, gardens, places, stalls)**
2. As they __________ at the market, the first thing people saw were the beautiful peaches. **(glanced, arrived, looked, peeped)**
3. "If I were to give you a peach, I would have to do the same for every __________." **(tramp, thief, man, person)**
4. How could you __________ this poor man? **(help, waste, deny, destroy)**
5. The monk __________ everyone to eat a peach. **(told, made, forced, asked)**
6. When the farmer discovered that all his peaches were gone, he was __________. **(amazed, happy, enraged, sorry)**

D

Choose the correct answer.

1. Where had the farmer grown his peach trees?

(a) In a small field.

(b) In a small yard.

(c) In a small garden.

(d) In a small greenhouse.

2. A monk approached the farmer just before

(a) morning. (b) midday.

(c) midnight. (d) evening.

3. Why did the old man buy the monk a peach?

(a) He felt sorry for the monk.

(b) He felt sorry for the farmer.

(c) He felt annoyed with the monk.

(d) He felt annoyed with the crowd.

4. Which sentence is true?

(a) He planted the plum stone in the ground.

(b) He planted the avocado stone in the ground.

(c) He planted the mango stone in the ground.

(d) He planted the peach stone in the ground.

5. Why did the farmer follow the monk?

(a) To demand thanks for his peaches.

(b) To demand money for his peaches.

(c) To demand his peaches back.

(d) To demand an apology.

E

Grammar

Rewrite the following sentences putting in the capital letters, full stops and question marks.

1. joe travelled from his tiny village of hao chu, in china
2. "where do I set up my stall" he asked
3. "could I have some water, please" the monk asked the crowd
4. the peach tree will have grown tall by monday
5. "can we each eat a peach" su yin asked the monk
6. by sunday evening the farmer was tired and weary

F

Explore the Text

The tone of the story "Talking Animals" in Unit 7 is funny.
What is the tone of this story? Give some reasons for your answer.

G

Use Your Imagination

Imagine you are the old man who was sitting near the barrow and observing all that happened. Write what you saw in your own words.